THE REVOLT OF THE WHIP

THE REVOLT OF
THE WHIP

Joseph L. Love

Stanford University Press
Stanford California

Stanford University Press
Stanford, California

Published with the assistance of the Edgar M. Kahn Memorial Fund.

Library of Congress Cataloging-in-Publication Data

Love, Joseph LeRoy, author.
  The Revolt of the Whip / Joseph L. Love.
    pages cm
  Includes bibliographical references and index.
  ISBN 978-0-8047-8106-0 (cloth : alk. paper) --
ISBN 978-0-8047-8109-1 (pbk. : alk. paper)
  1. Brazil--History--Naval Revolt, 1910. 2. Sailors, Black--Brazil--History. 3. Naval discipline--Brazil--History. 4. Race discrimination--Brazil--History. 5. Brazil. Marinha de Guerra--History. I. Title.
  F2537.L83 2012
  981'.05--dc23
                                    2011043060

Typeset by Bruce Lundquist in 10.9/13 Adobe Garamond

For Laurie
and the memory of Camille Bittick

Contents

Preface

Although I hope to bring new information and insights to the "Revolt of the Whip"—a spectacular revolt in the Brazilian navy by largely black crews against an all-white officer corps in 1910—I am writing for a primarily American audience. Such readers might wonder whether there are similar events in the history of the United States. Unsurprisingly, there are no precise parallels in the American experience to the events described in the following pages, but three incidents in our own history deal with similar racial themes on the high seas or in the US Navy. Two of them concerned uprisings of captives aboard slavers—in 1839 on *La Amistad*, a Spanish-chartered vessel, and in 1841 on the *Creole*, an American ship.[1] Both ended in court cases, the first in Connecticut, and the second on Nassau, in the Bahamas. Both, but especially the first, fired the abolitionist movement in the United States. In the *Amistad* case, ex-president John Quincy Adams defended the self-liberated slaves before the US Supreme Court, and Steven Spielberg told the story to the world in his movie *Amistad*. Though considered mutinies rather than cases of piracy, the *Creole* and *Amistad* incidents were revolts by captives rather than crew members, and in both instances the slaves ultimately walked free.

An incident more directly resembling the Brazilian rebellion occurred in World War II at Port Chicago, California. The mutiny there was more unambiguously a race-based rebellion than the Brazilian revolt studied here. Like the US Army, the navy had remained segregated throughout World War II. At Port Chicago the black seamen's assignment had been to load munitions onto cargo ships in the war against Japan. On July 17, 1944, a terrific explosion occurred at the loading dock: 320 men were killed, of which 202 had been black enlistees. Another 390 other men were injured; two-thirds of them were African Americans. These numbers amounted to 15 percent of all black casualties in World War II. The blast was equivalent to five kilotons of TNT, about one-third the force of the Hiroshima explosion. Port Chicago was the worst disaster on the American homefront during the war.

Blame was placed not on the white officers in charge of the loading, but on the black sailors who were killed.[2] Fearing another explosion, a seaman named Joe Small, who had been an informal broker between officers and men, led a work stoppage on August 9, 1944. As a result, 258 African Americans were imprisoned. Under threat of a charge of mutiny, four-fifths of the accused decided to return to work; despite this, all 258 were court-martialed. They were charged with mutiny, an offense that implies intent to take power, though their action was in fact a work stoppage to protest the perilous conditions in which they were forced to work. The sailors had no lawyers to represent them. The chief counsel of the NAACP, Thurgood Marshall—later to become the first African American on the US Supreme Court—took up their cause, although as a civilian, he could not represent them in a court-martial. Fifty men—those who had defied the threat of court-martial—were declared guilty of mutiny and sentenced to fifteen years' imprisonment. Punishments were subsequently reduced, but initially not that of Small and nine others. Following the United States' victory in the Pacific, Small and others were released in 1946 and discharged from the navy in July, two years after the "mutiny" at Port Chicago. Perhaps the perceived injustice in the handling of the Port Chicago rebels contributed to the navy's decision to abandon segregation in 1947; it was the first of the US armed services to do so.

Although the Brazilian revolt of 1910 occurred on ships afloat rather than loading docks, there were a number of similarities with the Port Chicago events. For one thing, both rebellions were implicitly working class. For another, the leaders of the Brazilian movement, like Joe Small, were older than their followers, but most, like Small, were still in their early twenties. And again, like the American Small, the three principal Brazilian leaders between them had sufficient skills and enough education and experience to earn the trust and obedience of their comrades. Furthermore, both Brazilian and American rebels were motivated by outrageous grievances—in the American case, the mass death of their fellows and the threat of impending death for the survivors, and in the Brazilian case, the persistence of flogging, associated with the recently abolished institution of slavery. To be sure, the Brazilian uprising was unique, and it played a memorable role in the history of resistance to oppression, not just of blacks, but of other lower-class people as well. In what follows I do not seek to create heroes or burnish the reputations of courageous men; some previous accounts have done this. Rather, my intention is to tell a good story, faithful to the known facts, about real people—sailors and the elites who ruled them—and their triumphs and failings.

Acknowledgments
and Spelling Conventions

As brief as it is, this book has a long history. I took my first notes for it in Paris at the Archives du Quai d'Orsay in 1982 [*sic*], while researching another subject. The notes went into a drawer for several years. I worked on the Brazilian sailors' revolt at moments snatched from other concerns over the following decades, when I happened to be in Rio de Janeiro, Lisbon, Washington, or London. The project became a kind of hobby, a word I prefer to "obsession." As the years went by, new materials became available and relevant new studies appeared. Even now, however, neither I nor other historians working on the revolt have explored all the relevant sources. Among other things, the reactions of the German and Argentine governments have yet to be adequately examined. In any event, like all researchers, I became indebted to a number of persons and institutions who helped me realize this project, minus the customary acknowledgment of foundation support that usually figures in such lists. Among those who helped me were fellow scholars interested in the revolt itself—Álvaro Pereira de Nascimento, Sílvia Capanema de Almeida, Zachary Morgan, Marco Morel, and Admiral Hélio Leôncio Martins. Others who assisted me at various times were two former students, Bert Barickman and Zephyr Frank, now colleagues. Dain Borges and Jeffrey Needell greatly improved the manuscript, whatever its present merits, by writing thorough critiques as anonymous readers. Michael Hall unfailingly offered good advice on sources and repositories. My research assistant, Noah Lenstra, helped me to organize the endnotes; he also standardized spelling and ordered the bibliographical materials, as well as combing through documents and using his skills in drawing maps and enhancing the quality of photographs.

I am grateful to the personnel of the following institutions that provided archival materials, published sources, cartoons, and photos: in Brazil, the Arquivo Nacional, the Biblioteca Nacional, the Arquivo da Marinha, the Museu da Imagem e do Som, the Arquivo Geral da Cidade do Rio de Janeiro, the Arquivo Público do Estado do Rio de Janeiro, the Asociação Brasileira da Imprensa, and the Casa Rui Barbosa (all in Rio), the Biblioteca Mário de Andrade in Sao Paulo, and the Arquivo Público do Estado do Rio Grande do Sul in Porto Alegre; in the United States, the National Archives and Records Administration in Washington, DC, and the Library of the University of Illinois in Urbana; in Britain, the National Archives in London; in France, the Archives Diplomatiques du Quai d'Orsay in Paris; and in Portugal, the Arquivo do Ministério de Negócios Estrangeiros in Lisbon.

Brazilian Portuguese orthography has undergone several reforms since the period studied here, and I have followed the widely accepted practice of using modern spelling in the text and original spelling in the list of works cited. The original orthography will be useful for students and scholars who want to check the sources I used.

Map of Guanabara Bay, 1910

THE REVOLT OF THE WHIP

§1 The Marvelous City and the New Navy

With its granite mountains rising from the sea, its seemingly endless beaches, and its new landscaping, Rio de Janeiro had no rival in tropical splendor during the Belle Époque. Following the abolition of slavery in 1888 and the replacement of the increasingly inert imperial regime by a federal republic in 1889, Brazil's leaders sought to catch up with Argentina, even surpass it, as a candidate member of the comity of "civilized" nations. Around 1890, Rio had lost its position as the largest city in South America to Buenos Aires, the Argentine capital, and many Cariocas (inhabitants of Rio) admired the metropolis of the Rio de la Plata. General Emídio Dantas Barreto, who plays a role in the narrative below, wrote of the Argentine metropolis in 1906, "Its avenues of luxurious palaces and its monuments, gracefully conceived in every detail, spoke to us of the wealth, taste, and culture of this hardworking and daring people who realized the ideal of progress and civilization in Spanish America."[1]

Other Cariocas imagined their city to be in fierce competition with Buenos Aires: the protagonist of a 1909 novel by Afonso Henriques Lima Barreto, the celebrated bohemian writer and social critic, summed up Cariocas' envy of the great city on the Rio de la Plata:

> We were weary of our mediocrity, our lassitude. The vision of a clean, attractive, and elegant Buenos Aires provoked us and filled us with a mad desire to equal it. In this [emotion] there was a looming matter of national amour-propre and a dimwitted yearning not to allow foreigners, on returning [to their countries] to pour forth criticisms of our city and our civilization. We envied Buenos Aires moronically. [The argument ran:] "Argentina shouldn't outshine us; Rio de Janeiro couldn't remain just a coaling station, while Buenos Aires

was a genuine European capital: Why didn't *we* have broad avenues, carriage drives, formal-dress hotels, and gambling casinos?"[2]

Yet in many ways the Cariocas' aspirations were already being met through advances in sanitation, public works, architecture, and the stylish display of wealth. By 1910, Brazil's capital had become the "Marvelous City" celebrated in the Carnival march of that name.[3] Dr. Oswaldo Cruz, a pioneer of preventive medicine for the tropics, had attacked bubonic plague in the city in the late 1890s, vastly reducing the number of cases by 1908, and eliminating the disease altogether in the following decade.[4] More spectacularly, Cruz had virtually freed Rio from yellow fever during the mosquito eradication campaign of 1907. In 1909 he declared Rio to be free of that illness.

The more salubrious city would attract new inhabitants, and by 1910 it would have 870,000 residents,[5] though Rio still trailed Buenos Aires. Although it might be said that the beautification of Brazil's capital dated from 1808, when the exiled Portuguese regent (the future João VI) commissioned the neoclassical Botanical Gardens, the city planners of the new Republic remade the face of the city. During the first years of the new century, Prefect Francisco Pereira Passos and his chief engineer Paulo de Frontin had overseen the redesign of the Brazilian metropolis, including the creation of its sinuous and sensuous Avenida Beira Mar (Seashore Drive). This thoroughfare connected the fashionable districts of Glória, Catete, Flamengo, and Botafogo to the commercial center of the capital, and the New Tunnel linked Copacabana to the established residential areas in 1906. Four years later, 615 licensed automobiles were cruising the city.

In the beachfront districts of Glória, Flamengo, and Botafogo, and soon in Copacabana too, *palacetes*, palatial multistory homes, were erected on the Beira-Mar in a style that might be called tropical gingerbread. They featured fanciful towers, arcades, and balconies fronting Guanabara Bay. The writer Lima Barreto even refers to a "Botafogo style" of *palacetes*, surrounded by iron fencing and featuring ornate plaster work and a veranda on the side.[6] Art Nouveau motifs were frequent.

Official Rio was also showing a new face. When it opened its doors in 1909 Brazil's premier theater, the Teatro Municipal, inspired by the Paris Opera, offered an adaptation of nineteenth-century French eclecticism coupled with modern ventilation.[7] The building displayed "a profusion of marble, velvet and gilding."[8] It was Brazil's answer to the great opera house of Buenos Aires, the Teatro Colón, which had opened a year earlier. The Teatro Municipal was situated on the Avenida Central, a motorway cutting a north-south line through the heart of downtown and stretching from today's Praça (square) de Mauá to the Praia (beach) de Santa Luzia, thus linking two distant points on the bay. City planner Frontin had purposely designed the Avenida Central to be thirty-three meters wide, so that its width would exceed that of the famed Avenida de Mayo in Buenos Aires by three meters.[9]

But the Teatro Municipal was hardly the only memorable state building erected on the Avenida Central in early years of the new century. Other notable institutions were the National Library, the National School of Fine Arts, and the Naval Club, inaugurated in May 1910 in the presence of President Nilo Peçanha. Designed by the Italian architect Tomasso Bezzi, the Club was richly appointed with marble columns and parquet floors. An official pamphlet describes it as constructed "in an eclectic style with elements of the Italian Renaissance," having "marine motifs" both inside and out.[10] In the Green Salon one can still see a painting of Brazil's first great battleships, the *Minas Gerais* and *São Paulo*, moving at full steam.

Among the stately new commercial buildings erected, slate-covered turrets and bell-shaped domes, topped with spires, abounded, though "most of the Avenida's construction involved a Beaux-Arts façade grafted on to a plain, functional building . . . a Brazilian body with a French mask."[11] By 1909, the city also had ten movie theaters, all concentrated on and near the Avenida Central. Meanwhile, the construction of the cable car to the top of Sugarloaf Mountain, the most famous of the Rio's granite *morros*, had been initiated in 1908 and would be completed in 1912. Rio's new port—financed, like so many public works—by foreign loans, opened the city to expanded trade and travel in 1910. At that time, it was the fifteenth most important port in the world in terms of freight handled.[12]

Traversing the Avenida Central was the cultural heart of the capital city, the Rua do Ouvidor, built in the mid-eighteenth century, but recently spruced up by the new premises of the traditional Garnier and Lammert book stores. On the Ouvidor, the city's most fashionable street, men could be seen in top hats at midday, while upper-class women more sensibly carried parasols. Most of the leading newspaper offices were located on the Ouvidor or the Avenida Central—among them *Jornal de Comércio* (the most respected daily), *O País* (the unofficial mouthpiece of the government), *Correio da Manhã* (the leading opposition paper), *Jornal do Brasil,*

Diário do Rio de Janeiro, and *Diário de Notícias*. Ouvidor was also the most stylish street for Carnival activities. The modern Carnival had arisen in the early years of the new century, as the samba replaced the *entrudo* as the leading street dance of Carnival on the Ouvidor and elsewhere in the years around 1910.[13] On an adjoining street, parallel to the Avenida Central, stood the city's best restaurant and tearoom, the Confeitaria Colombo, which survives to the present day. Laid out in Art Nouveau style, the Colombo had four floors appointed with countertops of Italian marble, eight three-by-six-meter mirrors set in jacarandá frames, and crystal chandeliers. An oval window of tiffany glass provided additional overhead light.

No one was more concerned with Rio de Janeiro's new glamour than the Brazilian foreign minister, the baron of Rio Branco, who was eager to display the city to the world. Rio Branco had hosted the third Pan-American Conference there in 1906,[14] making Rio de Janeiro the first city in South America to sponsor the event, ahead of Buenos Aires. The Monroe Palace,[15] a French eclectic extravaganza erected in 1904 to display Brazil's opulence and grandeur at the St. Louis World's Fair (Louisiana Purchase Exposition), was dismantled and reconstructed in Rio for the Pan-American Conference.[16] It was placed at the south end of the Avenida Central, where an obelisk was also raised to commemorate the whole complex of new buildings and landscapes associated with the creation of the *avenida*. In 1908 the Brazilian government put Rio on view again at Brazil's first National Exposition, commemorating the centenary of the arrival of the Portuguese royal court from Europe, a twelve-year exile that, in effect, had initiated Brazilian independence. (That the Exposition of 1908 would upstage Argentina's centennial celebration by two years could not have escaped Rio Branco.) An array of gleaming-white palaces, whimsically eclectic in design, was erected by Brazil's major states for the occasion.[17] Elsewhere, a pile similar to the Monroe Palace—also with imposing columns and slate dome—was raised for the Brussels World's Fair in 1910. The Argentinians meanwhile hosted their own international exposition in conjunction with their country's centenary of independence.

The *Povo*

Rio's new face could not mask an inconvenient reality: given that some very large share of the population of Rio de Janeiro and Brazil as a whole was nonwhite—perhaps half, though nobody knew for sure—and given that many, perhaps most, politically aware Brazilians tended to believe nonwhite populations were innately incapable of achieving the same level of development as white ones, how could Brazil succeed against Argentina or any other country perceived as white? The most widely accepted "solution" was that Brazil should adopt European ideas about lifestyles and attract European settlers on a massive scale, as Argentina had, and that continued race mixture and displacement over time would result in a benign whitening effect. In the meantime, in Rio poor people could be pushed into the background in the newly Europeanized capital. The same pushing would occur in other cities as well.

To an anonymous British observer of the era, Brazil was a country of "illiterates and *doutores*" (doctors, that is, university graduates).[18] In fact, in 1910 about three-quarters of the national population could not read. And though the rate of illiteracy was lower in the cities, behind the glittering new facade of Rio de Janeiro lay the city of the *povo* (the populace, lower classes), considerably more African in appearance, on the average, than the upper classes. As James Scott has noted about Brasília, officially inaugurated as Brazil's capital in 1960, the planned city and the unplanned slums it spawned were symbiotic;[19] such was the case of Rio before it. And the Marvelous City was not created without social cost. The urban planners of the early twentieth century wanted foreign visitors to see a predominantly Europeanized and prosperous Rio de Janeiro, an objective achieved by leveling tenements and slums near the center of the city, which such visitors were most likely to see. Just to build the Avenida Central and remodel the areas alongside it, 640 buildings, many of them tenement houses, were razed, and their lower-class inhabitants were forced to seek shelter elsewhere.[20]

The Republican regime also introduced new measures of social control. A long-term process that began in 1889 and was virtually completed twenty years later was the suppression of *capoeira* (hooligan) gangs.[21] The first chief of police under the republic, João Baptista Sampaio Ferraz, made this task a priority since former slaves, some of whom had only been freed in 1888, were drifting into the capital city in large numbers. By 1910, the problem of gangs was largely limited to roving street urchins.[22] Furthermore, in Pereira Passos' new urban order, beggars, vagrants, and prostitutes were to be kept out of public spaces.[23]

The *povo* had rioted against compulsory smallpox vaccination in 1904, and in response, Justice Minister J. J. Seabra had ordered a broad sweep of the capital city.[24] "Jacobin" followers of Marshal Floriano Peixoto, led by a former military officer and former governor of Pará, Lauro Sodré, tried to use the crowd to topple the government of President Rodrigues Alves and found support among cadets at the Military School at Praia Vermelha.[25] Almost a thousand people were arrested, half of whom were soon released. The rest were removed from Rio. Foreigners, labor activists, and people among the poorest sectors of the population were first detained at the Ilha das Cobras (Snake Island), under the jurisdiction of the navy. From there, Brazilian nationals were sent to the farthest reaches of the newly acquired Amazonian Territory of Acre, and noncitizens were deported.[26] The latter element, which constituted about 25 percent of the city's population, was considered to be a special problem, despite the fact that the largest group among them was the Portuguese, who were most easily assimilated.[27] Among the non-Brazilians were prostitutes of all classes, pimps, and labor agitators, especially anarchists, but socialists and communists as well.[28] In 1907 the Adolfo Gordo Law granted the state broader powers to rid itself of criminal and politically radical foreigners. In addition, roundups across the city to remove domestic and foreign undesirables were facilitated by repeated proclamations of a state of siege in 1904–5, and every year from 1909 through 1918, excepting only 1915–16.[29]

Nor did the populace of the capital city have effective political rights. Only literate males age twenty-one and older could vote, and political enforcers linked to the government under the president's appointed prefect kept the turnout low. In the early years of the republic, as in the late empire, the police used their own *capoeiras* to break up the meetings of the opposition candidates and to intimidate their followers at the polls, a process simplified by the fact that votes were cast by open ballot.[30] Despite the much higher literacy rate in Rio than in the country as a whole, only 2.8 percent of the total population in the capital city was registered to vote in 1910. In the presidential election that year, less than 0.5 percent of the city's population actually cast valid ballots. Yet in the country as a whole, 2.7 percent cast such ballots—seven times as many as in Rio. Of the total number of registered voters, those who cast certified votes numbered only a little more than half the national average, raising the suspicion of massive fraud.[31] "It can be said that the republic almost literally eliminated . . . the right of political participation through the vote" in the capital city, in the view of the historian Murilo de Carvalho.[32] A contemporary witness, the French ambassador stated that four-fifths the voting stations in Rio were closed down by the police during the presidential elections of 1910.[33]

An observer who frequently crossed the line between the elite and the *povo* was the journalist Paulo Barreto, better known by his pen name, João do Rio. The city's best-known *cronista* (chronicler of daily events and gossip columnist), João do Rio was also the city's leading *flaneur*. His *Enchanting Soul of the Streets*, published in 1908, brought together the writer's observations on the bizarre and remarkable inhabitants of the city.[34] They included professional prayer-chanters and mourners, street artists, *cordões* (predecessors of modern samba schools), street balladeers, whose moralistic tales in verse resembled those of today's *literatura do cordel*, occupants of flophouses, beggars learning their profession, prisoners, and tattoo artists. According to João do Rio, the majority of lower-class Cariocas were tattooed. The *cronista* mentions an astute sailor named Joaquim, who had a crucifix tattooed on his back to lessen the possibility that he would be whipped by his superiors.[35]

The Political Elite

Upper-class Cariocas were not especially proud of the lower orders that João do Rio described, and they probably considered the people he wrote about weird and dangerous. The political elite, like the broader social elite from which it was derived, tended to be Caucasian in appearance, though the standards for "whiteness" were more relaxed as one moved along the coast north of the Federal District, containing the city of Rio de Janeiro. To be sure, it was not the case that persons with African forbears were excluded from middle and upper strata of Carioca society, so long as they spoke and wrote Portuguese correctly and had the appropriate manners and values. In the absence of a "white" reality, which Brazilians assumed Argentina enjoyed, Brazilian society was inclusionary of non-whites who accepted European (and especially French) values and symbols of civilization.

Despite their doubts about the extent to which their nation could claim European descent, middle- and upper-stratum Brazilians were eager to stake out a place for their country on the international scene. Although the political elite and the broader social elite felt sure of their right to rule those beneath them, they were less certain about the degree to which their nation cut a figure on the world stage. They were proud of the inventor Alberto Santos Dumont, who was arguably the first man to fly an airplane, based on his experiments in Paris in 1906. Brazilians were also proud of the role that Senator Rui Barbosa, the country's leading legal mind, had played at the Second Hague Peace Conference in 1907. Though less well known, the fact that Brazil had won a gold medal at the International Hygiene Congress, also in 1907, reflected the impressive achievements in public health of Oswaldo Cruz. His research laboratory for tropical medicine at Manguinhos, a Rio suburb, would identify new diseases in the future.[36]

Brazilians were also proud of their foreign policy achievements, especially under Foreign Minister José Maria da Silva Paranhos Jr., better known by his imperial title, the baron of Rio Branco. The scion of the viscount of Rio Branco, the prime minister who had begun the emancipation of slaves in 1871, the baron grew up in the most intimate circles of power-wielders in imperial Brazil. Born in Rio in 1845 but with roots in Bahia, he attended the empire's most prestigious secondary school, the Colégio Pedro II, named for Brazil's second emperor. The youth subsequently entered the law school at São Paulo, but graduated from Brazil's other college of law at Recife. Studying at both academies was a means of insuring that he would make the acquaintance of the majority of the political actors of his generation. After a short stint as a member of the Chamber of Deputies and still in his twenties, Rio Branco assisted his father in drawing up the peace treaty with Paraguay, which Brazil, together with Argentina and Uruguay, had defeated in South America's bloodiest nineteenth-century war, from 1864 to 1870. (Brazil had been the leading combatant among the three allies and occupied the conquered country.) The future baron became a full-time diplomat in 1876, taking a consular post in Liverpool. He distinguished himself in several European posts and was ennobled by the emperor in the dying days of the old regime. Despite his monarchist convictions, Rio Branco continued his diplomatic career during the republic, and served as ambassador to Berlin in 1900. President Rodrigues Alves appointed him minister of foreign relations in 1902.

On his way to the top post in the Foreign Ministry, Rio Branco had won important territorial awards from France in a region bordering French Guiana, and from Argentina in the Missões [Misiones] District, in negotiations arbitrated by then US president Grover Cleveland. Backed by Brazil's superior naval power, Rio Branco as foreign minister won the territory of Acre from landlocked Bolivia in 2003, following a revolt in the disputed territory by the Brazilian filibuster Plácido de Castro. It was Rio Branco who announced the enormously expensive naval rearmament program in 1904.[37]

Rio Branco was portly but imposing, with his diplomat's cutaway and walrus moustache. He had a scholarly bent as well, and part of his diplomatic success derived from his publication of multivolume works documenting Brazil's claims to regions in dispute with other countries, such as the seven-tome work defending Brazilian claims in Amapá against France. During his tenure at the Foreign Ministry, Brazil was honored in 1905 when Pope Pius X named Joaquim Arcoverde as the first cardinal in Latin America. The baron's prestige was such that he served continuously as foreign minister under four presidents, only vacating the office on his death in 1912. Two years later, the elegant Avenida Central in the capital was renamed the Avenida Rio Branco.

While Rio Branco skillfully distanced himself from the rough-and-tumble of the political process, not so the above-mentioned Rui Barbosa, senator from Bahia. A man of enormous erudition, oratorical skill, and legal talent—and like Rio Branco, a member of the Brazilian Academy of Letters—Rui was also adept at presenting an image to the public that glorified his achievements. Four years younger than Rio Branco, he shared with the diplomat the rare privilege of studying at both of the empire's law schools—the one at Recife and the other at São Paulo. Rui Barbosa had been a prominent opponent of slavery in the final years of the empire, and he had been one of the few civilians who had participated in the bloodless coup against the old regime in 1889. Rui, as he was usually known, had dominated the provisional government of Brazil's first president, Marshal Deodoro da Fonseca, as minister of finance. But many influential Brazilians, as well as foreign lenders, held Rui responsible for Brazil's financial collapse and the ensuing depression of 1891. In the struggle against Marshal Floriano's government in 1893, the Bahian senator supported the naval rebellion and was forced into exile in September.

Rui was one of the first Republican statesmen to champion a strong navy for Brazil. He was in England in 1895 when he published "Lesson of the Far East," arguing that Japan had soundly defeated China in their war of 1894–95 because of Japanese naval strength.[38] Back in Brazil under President Prudente, Rui resumed his place in the Senate and tended to take the high ground in congressional debates on political ethics; this posture suited his situation as a statesman at odds with the political establishment. He denounced the evils of providing public employment for relatives and other protégés, but he engaged in these practices himself, as did all other politicians of his era. Rui Barbosa enjoyed a lucrative law practice defending clients with big pocketbooks, such as Canadian Light and Power, the monopoly utility company in the national capital.[39]

Rui deservedly earned a reputation for political courage and legal erudition, and he scored a major publicity coup by hiring a British journalist to write a glowing account of his performance in 1907 at the Second International Peace conference at the Hague. The leading figure at the conference was the German diplomat and jurist Baron Adolf Marschall von Bieberstein, who successfully opposed any practical measures to limit armaments of the world's major states, an achievement of especial importance for Europe's chief military power, imperial Germany.[40] But in the account of William T. Stead, paid for by Rui, the Brazilian delegate cut the most impressive figure for his vast knowledge of international law and foreign languages. "Europe bowed before Brazil," according to the image Rui succeeded in establishing for himself. Rui was "the Eagle of the Hague." Privately, von Bieberstein, whose eminence Stead acknowledged, wrote that Rui Barbosa was the "most boring" figure at the event.[41] All the same, three years later, in 1910, the Brazilian orator and statesman, now the hero of aspiring youth, threw himself into a race for the presidency.

In this, the first contested presidential election in the country's history, the Bahian senator's opponent was the nephew of the man Rui had served in 1889–91. Hermes da Fonseca was a marshal of the army. Six years Rui Barbosa's junior and a decade younger than Rio Branco, Hermes da Fonseca had been born in São Gabriel, Rio Grande do Sul, where his officer-father was stationed in a frontier area near Uruguay. His father, like his uncle Deodoro da Fonseca, would later become a marshal in the Brazilian army. Like Rio Branco, Hermes attended the Colégio Pedro II, the elite preparatory school in Rio de Janeiro. His favored status was further indicated by the fact that he was chosen as the adjutant of the Conde d'Eu, consort to the heir apparent to the Brazilian throne, Dom Pedro's daughter Isabel. In the first year of the republic, 1890, Hermes was twice promoted—first to major and then to lieutenant-colonel. As a loyalist to the government of Floriano Peixoto, Hermes held the key post of commander of artillery in Niterói, facing the capital across Guanabara Bay. In 1900 he was promoted to brigadier. Three years later he was selected to head the police brigade in Rio, and in 1904, he became commander of the Tactical War School at Realengo, near Rio. In that position, Hermes rose to national prominence by suppressing the coup d'etat against President Rodrigues Alves in the revolt against compulsory vaccination. On this occasion, as in other crises, Hermes displayed a cool head. As a result of his actions, the grateful president promoted the soldier to marshal of the army.

Hermes da Fonseca also had considerable administrative abilities, and President-elect Afonso Pena named him minister of war in 1906, with a mandate to reorganize Brazil's army. In his ministerial capacity, Hermes reorganized and reequipped the Brazilian military, introducing a draft by lottery in 1906.[42] In the same year, he organized Brazil's "first large-scale field exercises" near Rio, attracting attention of the press.[43] Congress ratified his reforms and made new funds available for modernization. Hermes's administrative skills raised the army's morale to new heights, after the demoralizing "victory" of 1897 at Canudos, Bahia, where backlands millenarians had turned the army back three times before they were massacred.[44]

Hermes, with his cleft chin and perfect posture on foot or astride a horse, was the model of a "parade" general. His upwardly turned moustaches were perhaps fashioned in imitation of those of Kaiser Wilhelm, though probably with less wax. At any rate, Hermes seemed to be the sort of leader the Brazilian public could be proud of. Yet like Deodoro da Fonseca, Hermes notably lacked political aplomb. This, despite his demonstrated administrative talent and his close ties with important statesmen. One of these was Foreign Minister Rio Branco, who, ever attentive to opportunities for enhancing Brazil's international prestige, informed the marshal that he would be the first person in the Western Hemisphere to attend the military maneuvers of the German imperial army. It was no coincidence that the Brazilian government chose to contract German military advisors, to the consternation of the French.[45]

Brazil's first competitive presidential race in 1910 had its origin in a disagreement on succession between the Republican Parties of Brazil's two most populous and politically important states, São Paulo and Minas Gerais.[46] In the event, the São Paulo machine opted to support Rui Barbosa (not incidentally representing Bahia, the third most important state in population), with the governor of São Paulo, Manuel Albuquerque Lins, as his running mate. Meanwhile Minas's party supported Hermes, with Governor Venceslau Brás of Minas Gerais as his vice presidential nominee. In the understanding of the Brazilian public, just as Rui Barbosa had impressed the international community at the Hague, so Hermes had apparently done so in reorganizing the army. The French ambassador noted this perception among politically aware Brazilians and remarked to the French foreign minister that "the dominant trait of the Brazilian character [is] to appear." That is, to appear to be something one is not.[47]

Earlier in the new century, Brazil's Congress had fallen under the control of Rui's colleague in the Senate, José Gomes Pinheiro Machado, representing Rio Grande do Sul, Brazil's southernmost state. During the government of President Afonso Pena (1906–9), Pinheiro had obtained control of the credentials committees of both Chamber and Senate. Under Pinheiro's guidance, the Riograndense state machine backed Hermes, a native son of Rio Grande, for the presidency. Meeting at Pinheiro's home on the Morro (granite hill) da Graça in the fashionable district of Laranjeiras on May 14, 1909, the Riograndense and Mineiro Republican Parties arrived at a winning electoral combination. While the Mineiros represented the "oligarchy" representing coffee-export interests, Rio Grande's ranching economy was focused more on the domestic market, and its political elite professed allegiance to a certain form of Comtian positivism, to which many army officers across the country adhered. The action of the two state-based Republican Parties ruptured the São Paulo-Minas alliance, the united front of the two leading coffee-producing states, which also accounted for the largest vote totals. In third place was Rio Grande do Sul: Pinheiro's state party proved itself more powerful and cohesive in 1910 than its counterpart in Rui's Bahia. Because suffrage was limited to literate adult males, Rio Grande could marshal more votes than Bahia in the direct presidential elections, despite its smaller population.[48] Pinheiro used his power to validate the vote-counting in the presidential election of March 1910. He was even able to deny Rui a majority in his native state, Bahia, by manipulating local and regional political bosses, who controlled the vote tabulation and validation.[49]

Rui Barbosa had made the election of 1910 an issue of civilian versus military rule, and following his overwhelming but fraud-contaminated defeat in March, he continued to lead the congressional opposition against Hermes after the latter's inauguration in November.[50] Meanwhile, Pinheiro had organized a coalition of state parties at the national level, one he called the Conservative Republican Party (Partido Repúblicano Conservador, or PRC).[51] It would back the president's program of continued military and naval expansion, begun in 1906 under President Pena.

Since Pinheiro Machado and Hermes da Fonseca both hailed from Rio Grande, it is not surprising that their careers had been intertwined in a state proud of its military heritage on Brazil's southern frontiers, where all Brazil's foreign wars had been fought. Pinheiro had even obtained the rank of general through his military services in suppressing rebel forces during the civil war of 1893–95. The closeness of the Pinheiro-Hermes relationship is indicated by the fact that the marshal served as a second in a duel Pinheiro fought in 1906.[52] He was now consolidating his power behind the throne of a military president whose political skills could be likened to those of the feckless Ulysses S. Grant (US president, 1869–77).

Although of only average height, Pinheiro Machado had a penetrating gaze and a commanding presence, complemented by his curly grey locks, aquiline nose, and coal-black moustache. He might be compared to an American leader of a generation later than his own, Lyndon Johnson. Both hailed from states with famous ranching traditions, and both were masters of the upper chamber of their respective legislatures. Both were dominating personalities, and neither was averse to using political office for personal gain. More than the Texan Johnson, however, Pinheiro would dress the part of the cowboy if it suited his political purpose. Like Johnson, Pinheiro came from a political family. He was the son of a rancher who had represented Rio Grande do Sul in the Imperial Chamber of Deputies. The son was a graduate of the prestigious law school at São Paulo and a veteran of both the Paraguayan War and the civil war against the "federalists" (former Liberals) in 1893–95, when he was wounded and rose to the rank of general.

Mixing easily with different social strata, along the Uruguayan and Argentine frontiers Pinheiro spoke Spanish to the gauchos.[53] (In fact, Riograndenses were also known as *gaúchos*.)[54] Nor did the senator hesitate to take his peers' money in a friendly game of poker. As for financial scruples, according to one observer, Pinheiro had amassed an "improvised fortune," but he wasn't "precisely a dishonest man. Rather, he was a born deal-maker, and with that temperament never missed a chance for a profitable transaction."[55]

Pinheiro Machado enjoyed watching a cockfight, but among his friends in the Senate was the cultured Rui Barbosa.[56] He told his young acolyte Gilberto Amado, a reporter for the establishment newspaper, *O País*, "When Rui speaks, I become more intelligent; he says what I wish I could say." Rui "has more courage than talent," Pinheiro exclaimed, adding, "if that's possible."[57] Pinheiro Machado himself was fearless. Not only did he fight duels, but he habitually carried a silver-plated Smith & Wesson revolver on his person. Pinheiro had contempt for the *povo*, who saw in him the power behind Hermes's throne, and he defied the crowds that jeered him as his automobile passed through the capital.

Despite his remarks about Rui Barbosa, Pinheiro Machado was said to have the bad habit of treating his peers in the Senate and President Hermes with the same familiarity he accorded his ranch hands. He addressed the president as "Siu [*sic*] Hermes [Mister Hermes]."[58] He addressed political aspirants as "Vosmecê," a kind of mock formalism at a time when "você" had already become the standard polite form of the second person. Many political decisions were made in the senator's billiard room, and when Pinheiro lined up a shot, "[all] Brazil was suspended on that cue," wrote Amado of his former patron. Amado marveled at the "rapture with which the majority of those present communed in that ritual of adulation, their eyes raised toward Pinheiro."[59]

The Ships

Pinheiro Machado, using his influence in Congress, worked with Rio Branco to extend Brazil's international projection. Rio Branco's diplomacy in South America depended on the effective deployment of the army, but relied as well on that of the navy, and not only on the high seas: the navy had played a crucial role in the War of the Triple Alliance against Paraguay, fighting major battles on the Paraguay River and its tributaries at Humaitá and Riachuelo. More recently, it intervened in westernmost Amazonia, in 1902–4, during which Brazil sent naval vessels to support the rebellion in the Bolivian frontier region of Acre. As indicated, that area was quickly incorporated into Brazil, in the country's last territorial acquisition.

Beginning in 1904, furthermore, both the army and the navy undertook costly modernization programs, and most of the navy's outlays concerned the purchase of state-of-the-art naval vessels.[60] The program was initiated in the year in which the Japanese navy decisively defeated its Russian antagonist in the Tsushima Straits.[61] In this battle Japan had established the importance of combining superior armor, firepower, and speed in conflicts between opposing battleships. Tsushima stiffened the British navy's resolve to develop a new type of warship, in order to face its most likely enemy, the German imperial navy. Both the United States and Germany were closing on England in naval power, and in 1906 the British government took the decisive step of withdrawing its New World fleet from Bermuda, a move that implicitly conceded future hegemony in the Western Hemisphere to the United States.[62] At the end of the following year, President Theodore Roosevelt sent his Great White Fleet around the world, reaching Rio de Janeiro in January 1908. This assemblage of ships, consisting of four squadrons of four battleships each, alerted the Brazilians to an incipient shift in the balance of naval power.[63] Thus Britain, still in possession of the world's most powerful navy, had chosen to focus on the German challenge. The British henceforth would concentrate their naval forces in the North Atlantic and at strategic points along their Mediterranean and ocean routes to India, the "jewel in the crown" of the empire.

In 1906, the same year the fleet was withdrawn from Bermuda, British shipyards had produced a revolutionary warship—the *Dreadnought*, which also lent its name to a new class of battleships. This ship combined firepower, speed, and armor in a manner hitherto unknown. This was the first "all big-guns-ship," having no small caliber weapons and having double the number of cannon on previous large warships. The designers focused on the "main armament, magazines, and . . . turbine engines." The *Dreadnought* made other battleships obsolete and "became a symbol of a state's international standing, whether or not it served any national purpose."[64]

One of the *Dreadnought*'s supposed advantages was its beam (maximum breadth) of 83 feet, a size so great that, should the Germans have built a similar ship, it would be too wide to use the Kiel Canal, by which the imperial German fleet communicated between the Baltic and North Seas. All the same, the German navy quickly followed the British lead in dreadnought construction, and widened the Kiel Canal for that purpose.[65] The article "Navy and Navies," in the classic 1910–11 edition of the *Encyclopedia Britannica*, implied that Britain could not continue its policy of maintaining a navy equal to that of the next two powers combined.[66] The twentieth-century naval race was on, and it would soon involve all the Great Powers and lesser ones as well.

Brazil was among the latter countries. Its navy, like its army, had lost power and prestige during the 1890s: the army, because of its incomprehension of, and repeated defeats by, the millenarian movement at Canudos in 1896–97; the navy, because of sharp cleavages within the officer corps in the naval revolts of 1891 and 1893. Admiral Custódio de Melo had led the successful revolt against Deodoro's attempt to consolidate his dictatorship in November 1891,[67] but two years later that same officer's attempt to overthrow Fonseca's successor, Marshal Floriano Peixoto, ended in defeat. This outcome left the navy divided between *florianista* Republicans (some of them "Jacobins"), on the one hand, and conservative Republicans and monarchists, on the other. Eighty-three officers had been branded deserters in the civil war of 1893–95, in which naval rebels fought alongside provisional forces of excluded ranching elites, some of them monarchists, in Rio Grande do Sul. Floriano's successor, the civilian politician Prudente de Morais, had declared his intention to reorganize the navy, but he provided no funds for that purpose. In 1896, the money-starved navy only filled 45 percent of its authorized positions, a figure down from 98 percent in 1888.[68]

Morale rose markedly in both armed services in the twentieth century, because of vastly increased funds for new equipment and training. In 1904, the first year of a naval modernization program designed to last six to eight years, the minister of the navy and former *florianista*, Júlio César de Noronha, asked Congress to purchase new battleships not exceeding 13,000 tons.[69] But these orders were cancelled after Brazilian authorities learned of Argentina's plans to purchase a ship of 16,000 tons.[70] In any event, the 13,000-ton figure was deemed wholly inadequate after the arrival of the dreadnought class of ships. In 1905, word had reached the Brazilian admiralty of the coming of the dreadnought, and Minister Noronha revised his plans.[71] The naval purchasing program already authorized by the Brazilian Congress was expanded to include the purchase of two, and eventually three, of the great battleships that were the new gold standard of modern naval warfare. Because the ships were enormously expensive, a propaganda campaign had been necessary to secure the requisite appropriations by the Brazilian Congress. In addition, naval officers, backed by nationalist sympathizers, organized a naval league. The Liga Marítima Brasileira was a well-organized lobby formed in imitation of naval leagues in Britain and elsewhere.

The Brazilian government decided to purchase two fighting ships from British shipyards that were much more formidable than those originally contemplated of 13,000 tons' displacement. In November 1906, the Brazilian navy, the foreign service, the press, and congressional enthusiasts combined to expand the rearmament program far beyond the 1904 levels, thus initiating a South American arms race.[72] The almost unanimous support in the Senate was orchestrated by Senator Pinheiro Machado and the new minister of the navy, Alexandrino de Alencar, who, unlike Noronha, had been a rebel in 1893, and who was the author of the 1906 plan.[73] Pinheiro and Alencar, two Riograndenses who had fought on opposing sides in the civil war of 1893–95, were now close allies. Pinheiro had also authorized a series of frothy pronavy propaganda articles in the *Jornal do Comércio* by the journalist Augusto Souza e Silva.[74]

The new, expanded budget included three latest-model battleships of 19,280 tons; three rapid cruisers of 3 to 3.5 thousand tons; fifteen torpedo-cruisers of 600 tons; a mine layer; and three submarines. The dreadnoughts would have a speed of 21 knots per hour. In February 1907, Minister Alencar had negotiated a contract for three ships. Souza e Silva, the enthusiastic naval booster in the *Jornal de Comércio*, predicted that with its three dreadnoughts, only England, the United States, and Germany would be able to outgun Brazil.[75] With this nucleus of three ships, by adding another every two or three years (!), Brazil would soon have a squadron strong enough "to offer an effective guarantee of peace and good international relations," even if Argentina developed a similar squadron.[76] He did not explain the reasoning by which he reached this conclusion.

In the 1911 edition of the *Encyclopedia Britannica*, the first of Brazil's twin vessels, the *Minas Gerais*,[77] was the only battleship of which both a photograph and a diagram were included under the entry "Ship." It was the largest warship ever constructed in Britain or anywhere else.[78] On its initial test run at the Armstrong naval yards at Newcastle-upon-Tyne,[79] the *Minas Gerais* took on five hundred tons of coal, and seven hundred people boarded—engineers of the Armstrong company, machinists and boiler workers, plus Brazilian officers, engineers, and crewmen. The two alternating engines of 23,500 horsepower each moved converging propellers. There were eighteen Babcock and Wilcox boilers, plus two auxiliary boilers. Assuming a speed of ten knots per hour, the ship would have a range of almost ten thousand miles without having to refuel.[80] As part of their state-of-the art technology, the ships would be supplied with radio telegraphy, including the creation of such facilities ashore in the principal forts.

The new dreadnoughts cost the Brazilian government, in dollars of the day, ten million each.[81] These outlays, together with the costs of other ships in the new squadron, made the navy's expenditures jump from 54 percent of the army's budget in 1905 to 87 percent in 1910.[82] There to witness all the tests was the skipper-designate of the *Minas Gerais*, Commander[83] João Batista das Neves.[84] In all, 730 people had boarded, including 110 Brazilians.[85] The *Minas Gerais* had twelve 12-inch (305 mm) guns, with the ability to fire in a 360-degree radius; it could fire ten guns broadside, eight ahead and as many astern. (By comparison, the famous Russian battleship *Potemkin* had only four 12-inch guns.)[86] Moreover, the new ship had fourteen 4.7-inch (120 mm) cannon and armor varying from eight to nine inches' thickness, made by Krupp.[87]

From the British perspective, the naval armaments industry was big business, led by the firms of Armstrong and Vickers. Of the various kinds of battleships sold abroad between 1900 and 1914, Britain produced eighteen out of twenty-nine; the other exporting countries—Germany, the United States, France, and Italy—accounted for less than 10 percent of the market each, while Britain sold 62 percent.[88] Brazilian government officials may have been persuaded in part by British firms' bribes to switch from the 1904 naval program to the much larger one in 1906, including the dreadnoughts.[89]

The *Minas Gerais* and her twin, the *São Paulo*, were almost 1,400 tons heavier than the original *Dreadnought*. They were 500 feet long, the equivalent of almost two football fields. Each had a beam of 83 feet (the same as the original *Dreadnought*), and a draft of 25 feet. They could attain a maximum speed of 21 knots (24 mph; 39 km/h). Each displaced 21,200 tons of water. The ships would be fully staffed with 106 officers and 887 men each.[90]

At the end of 1910, according to *The Times* of London, Great Britain had twelve dreadnoughts and the rest of the Great Powers had thirteen, of which five belonged to Germany, and four to the United States, in third place.[91] But at that moment Brazil had two of the latest and largest dreadnoughts afloat. And still building in Britain was the mammoth *Rio de Janeiro*. She would not be 500, but 655 feet long, with a 92-foot beam; further, the monster ship would have a 26-foot draft and a displacement of 32,000 tons. The *Rio de Janeiro* would have twelve 14-inch guns and would achieve a maximum speed of 22.5 knots per hour, powered by 45,000-H.P. engines. She was to cost Brazil the unheard-of sum of three million pounds sterling (US$14,580,000).[92]

Brazil's two new capital ships in 1910 had more cannon and firepower than any previous ship afloat.[93] For "several years," Souza e Silva boasted—inaccurately, as it turned out—that the *Minas Gerais* [and the *São Paulo*] "would be the most powerful warship[s] in the world." Writing in 1909, he went on to predict, again incorrectly, that in the next eight years it would be materially impossible to construct any ships that were decisively superior to the *Minas Gerais*.[94] In his gushy account, he seems to have forgotten the huge ship under construction, the *Rio de Janeiro*.

Brazil's new projection of naval power, not surprisingly, attracted the notice of Argentine statesmen and naval officers. In 1906 the Buenos Aires newspaper *La Prensa* alleged that the Brazilian navy could destroy its Argentine counterpart after the acquisition of the new ships.[95] Early in 1910 the Argentine Republic ordered two vessels, to be christened the *Moreno* and the *Rivadavia*, named for heroes of the independence struggle whose centenary was then being celebrated. Each would displace 28,000 tons of water; they would measure 578 feet in length and possess turbines of 40,000 H.P. They would have a 96-foot beam and cut a 27 1/2 foot draft. In all these measurements, they were to be larger than their two Brazilian counterparts. They would have a top speed was 22.5 knots, slightly faster than the *São Paulo* and the *Minas*. Both Argentine ships were to be constructed in the United States.[96] Thus Argentina had resoundingly entered the lists against Brazil. But if Argentina was contending for naval dominance, Chilean officers and politicians felt they had to follow and ordered a dreadnought.[97] Yet in the short term, Brazil would have the advantage of monopoly of tremendous firepower in the South Atlantic because the Argentine ships would only be available in late 1911 or 1912.

Great ships were part of the lore of Brazil's capital city. The journalist João do Rio has a chapter on popular painting in *The Enchanting Soul of the Streets*, in which he mentions that a large canvas in a bar he frequented showed "destroyers cutting through the dense blue sky with projections of colossal holophote lights." The picture was titled, "the vision of progress." In the same book, João do Rio notes that the explosion of the Brazilian ironclad *Aquidabã* in 1894 was sufficiently alive in popular memory to be the subject of a Carnival song around 1908.[98] And when the *Minas Gerais* reached Rio de Janeiro from Europe in 1910, it was the occasion of great national pride. The *Correio da Manhã*, an eight-column daily and the newspaper most often opposed to the government, covered the arrival of this "giant of the sea" to the exclusion of all other news on page one of its April 17 edition. The above-mentioned *litterateur* Gilberto Amado, as a reporter for *O País*, went to the bay to witness the ship's arrival on April 18. In a memoir, Amado stated that "all Brazil saluted . . . the colossus of the South American seas, . . . the concrete expression of the energy of the nation." Once inside the bar, the *Minas* sent a salvo saluting the large ships in Guanabara Bay, the *USS North Carolina* and the Austrian cruiser *Kaiser Karl VI*.[99] The foreign ships returned the greeting to the ship that represented for Amado "the new opulent and powerful Brazil, pursuing the path of progress and civilization."[100] To add to the pomp, the *Minas Gerais* had a band of Italian musicians aboard. On the same day that the *Minas* arrived, the observatory at Rio de Janeiro witnessed the passage overhead of Halley's comet, making its appearance after a seventy-five-year absence. Was it an omen of good fortune for Brazil?

The new battleships were only the core of a greatly expanded navy. In addition to the *Minas* and *São Paulo*, the Brazilian government ordered lesser ships in Britain as well. The *Bahia*, a 18,000-H.P. cruiser of the "Scout" class, was launched in January 1909, with 288 crewmen, ten 4.7-inch cannon, and six lesser ones. It had two above-water torpedo-launching tubes. In April, the *Rio Grande do Sul*, with the same specifications as the *Bahia*, followed. Both were incorporated into the Brazilian navy in 1910. The two scouts were four-fifths the length of the *Minas Gerais* and the *São Paulo*.[101] Beyond the new cruisers and dreadnoughts, torpedo-cruisers, a mine layer, and submarines were commissioned. Finally, two coastal battleships, the *Deodoro* and the *Floriano*, built at the end of the 1890s, were refitted.

Souza e Silva had asked in 1909: What sacrifices would this unprecedented naval program require? He answered, "Much less than a humiliating defeat," and no one doubted that he had Argentina in mind as the more-than-likely antagonist.[102]

Officers and Men

No official data exist for the class or racial structure of the whole of Brazilian navy in the First Republic,[103] but there is broad agreement that the officers were almost exclusively white (by Brazilian standards, anyway).[104] There is also a widely accepted view that naval officers were more frequently members of the Brazilian upper class than were army officers.[105] True, no one has proven this assertion, yet to attend the Naval Academy (Escola Naval), a young man needed a substantial income.[106] In any case, many officers in both army and navy were members of families with long traditions of military service, frequently dating from colonial times. And another thing was certain: there was a wide gulf between officers and men. It was extremely uncommon for ordinary sailors to rise above noncommissioned status. A rare documented case, unique in the heights he attained, was that of Antônio Joaquim, who ascended from cabin boy to lieutenant-captain (*capitão-tenente*), a position between first lieutenant and commander (*capitão de fragata*), the rank just below that of the commander of the largest warships, *capitão de mar-e-guerra*. This anomaly occurred in Brazil's most hard-fought war, that against Paraguay from 1864 to 1870, and Joaquim lost his life in the conflict. The fact that he was white may have been an unstated but requisite element in his rise from the ranks.[107]

The sailors were separated from their superiors not only by an inferior level of schooling; in most cases, the men lacked even basic literacy. They were also noticeably, often strikingly, of darker skin color than officers.[108] This was a mark of caste in a country that had only abolished chattel slavery in 1888, making Brazil the last nation in the Western Hemisphere to do so.

Although information on the racial composition of the ranks is highly subjective, a recent study for the year 1908 by Sílvia Capanema provides concrete information. She found that, among the 250 sailors studied (8 percent of the total number of enlisted men in that year), 12 percent were classified as blacks (*preto*), 57 percent were classified as mixtures of black and white (*pardo*), although "pardo" was a very subjective term and was multivalent.[109] Twenty-one percent were categorized as white (*branco*), and 10 percent "dark" (*moreno*). Stated otherwise, 79 percent were to some degree African-derived.[110] Less direct evidence supports this precise observation. Partial counts and an educated guess tend to agree. Two studies concerning the nineteenth-century navy give exact tallies for small samples of the rank and file,[111] and in 1911 an informed observer made a broad estimate for the whole navy.[112] That writer, an anonymous "officer of the navy" held that 50 percent of the sailors were *negros*, (dark blacks) 30 percent were *mulatos*, 10 percent were *caboclos* (men of white, black, and Indian stock), and 10 percent "white or almost white."[113]

Staffing the armed forces took a variety of forms in both the army and the navy, but most sailors were recruited through naval apprenticeship schools, or were forcibly recruited. No tabulations exist for the republic, but in the empire, between 1840 and 1888, more than 15,000 men served in the navy, and, of these, only 3 percent had enlisted voluntarily.[114] Behind all forms of recruiting stood the threat of impressment. During the empire crews had been completed by invading merchant ships and dragooning their sailors. As the minister of the navy frankly admitted in his annual report of 1911, under the empire, military recruitment had been the "terror of the male population" and was used not only to fill military needs, but widely used as well to settle personal scores. Moreover, the threat of impressment helped unpopular governments obtain electoral majorities. Even in the opening years of the republic, military bands would sometimes march through Rio to attract crowds, lure young men into the Naval Arsenal, and impress them.[115]

But manpower requirements for the navy in the republic were filled in large part by the government's apprenticeship schools, where foundlings were sent. All of Rio's unadopted male foundlings, plus male orphans at the city's Santa Casa de Misericórdia, the city's leading charitable institution, were sent to the navy. Many became apprentices at age fourteen. Youths registered there had to stay in the navy fifteen years, according to the 1907 recruiting law for the navy. Those recruited by force had to serve twelve years, and volunteers, only nine.[116] In addition, a lottery-based draft of sailors already serving in the merchant marine was introduced in 1903. This measure required three years of service and two in the reserves. This feature was retained in the 1907 law, excepting that all sailors now had to remain in the reserves for three years.[117]

Officers and the political elite, one might assume, had scant regard for the men, who, according to official reports in the nineteenth and early twentieth centuries, were recruited among "the dregs [*fezes*, literally, 'feces'] of the population"—a phrase used repeatedly by ministers and members of parliament.[118] The anonymous "officer of the navy," cited above, described the crews as arising from "the sewers of society," while the minister of the navy in 1911 alleged, with some exaggeration, that police lock-ups (*xadreses*) were the main source of naval recruiting.[119] In fact, the majority of the recruits were coming through the apprentice schools. And the training program was evolving. In 1907 Christian doctrine was eliminated from the curriculum, and programs in Portuguese and arithmetic were strengthened, at least in theory. Yet in an attempt to obtain systematic data on all the sailors in 1908, the new Bureau of Naval Identification still listed the level of instruction of many sailors as "none," meaning that the men in question were illiterate and unable to do simple arithmetic.[120]

§2 The Rebellion and its Resolution

Brazil's naval program and the country's modernization more generally depended vitally on foreign investment to finance infrastructure, both directly and through the sale of government bonds abroad. To reduce the hefty risk premium exacted by international capital, Brazilian statesmen wanted to avoid, or at least minimize, domestic political disturbances. If we may take the view of *The Economist* as indicative of British capitalists' attitudes before the 1910 election, Hermes, the military candidate, had been a threat to order: "Enormous amounts of British capital have been placed in Brazil, and should Marshal Hermes be elected, we must be prepared for the worst. . . . [His victory] would lead in all likelihood to revolution." Such opinions were apparently the cause of a fall in the value of Brazilian bonds on the London market.[1]

In fact, as Hermes took office in mid-November, 1910, not only were there issues of legitimacy arising from Brazil's first contested presidential election because Rui Barbosa challenged fraudulent vote-counting in congress; beyond that, events in two states highlighted the weaknesses of Brazilian federalism. In the State of Rio de Janeiro, President Nilo Peçanha had backed his favorite against that of the outgoing governor in December 1909. The result was a *duplicata*: the legislature split into two rump bodies, and each legitimated the mandate of opposing claimants to the governorship. The issue was finally resolved in December, when the president sent in the army, imposing a state of siege in Rio state, and gave his full support to Francisco de Oliveira Botelho. In October 1910, another crisis had arisen in Amazonas, where the incumbent governor had backed Rui for president. Senator Pinheiro Machado and the Nery family "oligarchy," which had long dominated state politics but was currently out of power, now decided to oust the incumbent governor by force. They induced local army and navy units to bomb Manaus, the state capital. The governor withdrew from the city, but pleaded for the support of outgoing President Peçanha against the rebels. Nilo complied and directed the army to reseat Governor Antônio Clemente Bittencourt. What had happened in Amazonas under Nilo would grow worse during Hermes's four years in office: military reformers across the country, calling themselves "salvationists," maneuvered to oust traditional oligarchies at the state level, while Pinheiro Machado pursued a policy of shifting alliances, siding with the group that he judged would strengthen his power in Rio.

Hermes in Lisbon

Governmental instability in the republic, however, had not begun with Hermes da Fonseca; it had surfaced intermittently throughout the first decade of the new regime. Therefore, to assure foreign creditors and investors, Manuel Campos Sales, president-elect in 1898, had paid a ceremonial visit to London before his inauguration, in search of good will and foreign investment. Marshal Hermes da Fonseca continued this tradition in 1910, with unexcelled panache: after visiting London, Berlin, and Paris, and being received by King George V, Kaiser Wilhelm II, and President Fallières, he boarded the new dreadnought *São Paulo* in Cherbourg on September 27, prior to his final European stop in Lisbon.

The Portuguese capital was in fact a frequent port of call for Brazilian warships. But these vessels played a role as well in the illegal transport of immigrants. The destroyer *Bahia*, just constructed as part of Brazil's naval rearmament plan, was one such ship. Before leaving Lisbon in June 1910, the *Bahia* had illegally taken aboard some seventy persons without documents, including Portuguese minors, military reservists, and possibly criminals. Fifteen others, fugitives from military recruitment, had boarded the new battleship *Minas Gerais* at Ponta Delgada, capital of the Azores, during the ship's maiden voyage. According to the Portuguese embassy in Rio, other Brazilian naval vessels had taken on Portuguese "passengers" in similar circumstances.[2] Stowaways in such numbers might seem to reveal the incompetence of the officers. There was, however, a very different explanation of the Portuguese "passengers": Brazilian naval officers accepted foreigners to make up for the chronically insufficient number of deck hands on the new ships. The captain of the *Bahia* on the voyage just mentioned reported that in Lisbon he had recruited sixty men who wanted to emigrate to Brazil.[3]

Such issues were presumably far from the thoughts of President-elect Hermes when the *São Paulo* entered Lisbon harbor to thunderous applause on October 1; there was no ship in the Portuguese navy that bore comparison to it. The Brazilian president-to-be was the guest of King Manuel II, who, as a Bragança, was a member of the same family that had provided Brazil with its two emperors, ruling in succession from 1822 to 1889.

O Século, Lisbon's leading daily, devoted the whole of its first page on October 1 to Hermes's arrival. So did *O Mundo* the following day.[4] But *O Mundo* was a Republican newspaper, and it used Hermes's presence to make propaganda for the Portuguese republic: let us repeat the cry, *O Mundo* editorialized in its October 3 edition, "Long Live President Hermes! Long Live the Republic! Long Live Brazil!"[5] The "Republic" in question was not only Brazil's, but the one the editors hoped would soon appear in Portugal. Their opportunity swiftly followed: the same day that *O Mundo* welcomed Hermes, a leading Republican politician, the physician Miguel Bombarda, was assassinated, thereby setting in motion a Republican plot that had been prepared in advance.

Meanwhile, at 2 p.m. on October 3, Hermes, a guest in the royal Palace of Belém, was received by King Manuel in the Paço (palace) das Necessidades. Three hours later, the king went aboard the *São Paulo* as the guest of Marshal Hermes and the ship's commander, Francisco Marques Pereira e Sousa. Whiskey toasts were exchanged. Manuel made a thorough inspection of the battleship and witnessed a display of gymnastics by the sailors. He then received a twenty-one-gun salute.[6] That evening Manuel and his court attended the banquet that Hermes offered them at the Belém Palace, held there because the Brazilian legation was too small for the occasion. Just after the king had formally thanked his Brazilian host for the honor, Manuel was handed a message that political disturbances were in progress in Lisbon. Visibly nervous, he made his excuses to Hermes and took his leave.[7] In fact, the king was anticipating a Republican uprising.

At 1 a.m. on October 4, a revolt did break out in Lisbon, and in this struggle, Portuguese naval officers and men played the leading role. Just as a Republican revolution had overthrown the Bragança monarch Pedro II in Brazil, so the same fate now befell his cousin. Manuel II of Portugal had only ascended to the throne in 1908, as the result of the assassination of his brother, Carlos I. Unlike their illustrious predecessor, Manuel the Fortunate (reigned 1495–1521), Manuel II might be styled the Unfortunate: born the very day the House of Bragança was overthrown in Brazil (November 15, 1889), he now fell victim to the same process in Portugal.

The role of the Portuguese navy in the Republican revolution was not limited to commissioned officers. Ordinary sailors in Lisbon also played a key role in the events of the day. Republican sentiment was strongest among enlisted men, sergeants, and lower-ranking naval officers, according to a standard account of the revolution.[8] Of particular importance were the sailors who overcame their superiors at the Naval Barracks in Alcântara, a Lisbon suburb; meanwhile, officers and men, fighting side by side on the cruisers *Adamastor* and *São Rafael,* bombed the King's residence, the Paço das Necessidades. On a third cruiser, the *Dom Carlos,* the crew revolted, and in a struggle that included a boarding party led by an insurgent officer, the ship's loyal commander was killed.[9] Rear Admiral Carlos Cândido Reis, a rebel officer commanding two thousand seamen, was ready to attack the Terreiro do Paço, the center of the city where the king was holding out, but an assault proved unnecessary.[10] Late in the morning, at a moment when the revolutionary movement seemed destined to failure, naval lieutenant Antônio Machado Santos forced the government to surrender. Thus fell one of Europe's oldest monarchies: it had endured seven and a half centuries. Just as the Republicans who overthrew the Brazilian empire had played the Marseillaise at their moment of triumph, so did their Portuguese counterparts twenty-one years later.

The Portuguese Revolution put the Brazilian President-elect in an embarrassing position. Hermes had been the house guest of King Manuel and had exchanged toasts with him in two palaces and on the *São Paulo.* Yet the new situation urgently required a new posture. So, on October 6, following the approval by outgoing President Peçanha and Foreign Minister Rio Branco in the Brazilian capital, the marshal welcomed the Provisional President of the Portuguese republic, Teófilo Braga, aboard the Brazilian battleship. Champagne toasts were exchanged.[11] Only three days earlier had King Manuel stood in Braga's place on the great ship.

The Portuguese Revolution had begun in part on the *Adamastor,* a ship that would play a role in subsequent events in Africa and possibly in Brazil.[12] It took its name from a mythical monster appearing in the Portuguese national epic, Camões's *Lusíadas,* published in 1572. Adamastor was the enemy of seafarers at the Cape of Storms (Good Hope) on the southern tip of Africa. The ship had been financed by popular subscription to restore national pride, after Britain's humiliation of Portugal in 1890. At that time the Portuguese government had wanted to unite Angola and Mozambique by occupying the inland territory between them, but that aspiration ran afoul of Cecil Rhodes's "Cape to Cairo" plans for the British empire. So Britain had issued an ultimatum to Portugal to cease forthwith its efforts to consolidate Portuguese Africa into one bloc, and the government of Prime Minister José Luciano de Castro immediately fell.

Six weeks after the Portuguese Revolution of 1910, the captain of the *Adamastor*, João Manuel de Carvalho, led the official Portuguese delegation to the inauguration of Hermes da Fonseca as president of Brazil. Hermes was sworn in on November 15, the anniversary of the Republican coup d'état twenty-one years earlier.

The Eruption

The Belle Époque was the age of sumptuous banquets and receptions, no less in Rio de Janeiro than in Lisbon. On November 22, a day of "magnificent" weather, reaching a maximum temperature of only 74 degrees farenheit,[13] the newly inaugurated president attended a reception in honor of his brother, Dr. João Severino da Fonseca Hermes.[14] Sponsored by Senator Pinheiro Machado and other establishment politicians, the event featured ladies with "rich toilettes" prepared for the occasion. The president arrived at 10:30 p.m. with officials from his civilian and military staffs, including the minister of war, Dantas Barreto. Pinheiro Machado made an "eloquent speech." An hour later, one of the two bands present played the march from "Tannhäuser," a suitably triumphalist composition, followed by voice and violin solos by French and Italian composers.[15]

Around 12 a.m., however, Hermes received a phone call from Vice Admiral Joaquim Marques Batista de Leão, the minister of the navy, informing the president of a major naval revolt. Was it directed by Admiral Alexandrino Alencar, the naval minister under outgoing President Peçanha, whom Hermes had not reappointed, as he had extended the appointment of Rio Branco? Their antagonism was long-standing: in 1893 Hermes had been a loyal supporter of Floriano Peixoto in the battle to control Guanabara Bay, and Alencar had captained the rebel battleship *Aquidabã*.

The president immediately put several political enemies under surveillance, presumably including Alencar and his former rival for the presidency, Rui Barbosa. Like King Manuel at the banquet Hermes had offered him in Lisbon six weeks earlier, the new president, after informing the minister of war of the crisis, left the festivities to attend to the looming and grave danger. If the new president had any singular quality, it was his imperturbability in the face of crisis. Meanwhile War Minister Dantas Barreto prepared gun batteries at key points around Guanabara Bay.[16] The strategic situation had changed since the 1893 revolt in that modern 10-caliber howitzers had been placed on the *morros*, and military and naval communications were facilitated by a radio transmitter on the *morro* called Babilônia, overlooking Botafogo. But shore batteries, one of which Hermes had commanded during the 1893 revolt, had not kept pace with the firepower of the great new battleships.

At 1:30 a.m. on the 23rd, Minister Leão met Hermes at Catete, the presidential palace, and told him that the crews of the battleships *Minas Gerais* and *São Paulo*, as well as the cruiser *Bahia*, had revolted in Guanabara Bay.[17] Also present were the minister of war, Dantas, and Senator Pinheiro Machado, leader of the ruling Partido Republicano Conservador. The rebellion had occurred immediately after the return of the captain of the *Minas* from a foreign ship. It would soon be learned that the *Deodoro*, an older battleship, was also in the hands of the rebels. Pinheiro Machado counseled caution, in order not to provoke an attack on the unprotected city. Naval Minister Leão, in the view of War Minister Dantas, seemed at a loss what to do.[18]

The Portuguese *Adamastor* was one of many foreign ships in Guanabara Bay in the week following Hermes's inauguration. Another was the French training cruiser, the *Duguay-Trouin*, named for a privateer-turned-naval captain who rose to admiral under Louis XIV. René Duguay-Trouin had captured the heavily fortified city of Rio de Janeiro in 1711 and had held its Portuguese governor for ransom. It was aboard his namesake ship that the commander of the *Minas Gerais* was to have his last meal. On the night of November 22, one week after Hermes's inauguration, the captain of the French ship had entertained several guests for dinner. One was France's ambassador to Brazil, Lacombe, and three Brazilian naval officers. One of them was Commander João Batista das Neves.[19] He was the captain of the *Minas Gerais*, and his subordinate, Second Lieutenant Armando Trompowsky de Almeida, was also present.[20]

At about 10 p.m., Neves and Trompowsky withdrew, the latter returning to shore by launch, and the captain of the *Minas* boarding his ship.

But Neves's duties were not finished that evening. After acknowledging the greetings of Lt. Álvaro da Mota e Silva, Neves retired to his cabin. At that moment, a sailor attacked the lieutenant with a bayonet. "The Revolt of the Whip" had begun.

Rebel crewmen started shouting, "Down with the lash!" and "Long live liberty!" Neves then emerged from his quarters, still dressed in coat-and-tails from his dinner engagement, but now carrying a sword and a revolver; he passed another pistol to a loyal sailor. The skipper then called his men to attention, but only some sixty obeyed. At that moment a sailor struck Neves with an iron bar, knocking him to the deck. The commander managed to rise, while Lieutenant Cláudio da Silva and a loyal seaman momentarily forced the mutineers to retreat. But one of the latter group bayoneted Silva and another, Vitorino Nicássio de Oliveira, shot him dead. Commander Neves was similarly dispatched by seaman José do Nascimento. After Neves had fallen, a sailor performed mock gymnastic exercises before the body, while another urinated on the corpse.[21] After a third mutineer, Ernesto Roberto dos Santos, stabbed Sgt. Francisco Monteiro de Albuquerque, a quartermaster, Nascimento finished him off too. Lt. Mário Lahmayer tried to leave the ship with a few loyalists, but he was shot after entering a launch. Another officer did successfully board a small boat. Rebel sailors were also killed in the conflict. When daybreak came, the rebels sent the bodies of Neves and others ashore in a launch, after having honored them on the ship. The red flag of rebellion, flying on the prow of the rebel-held ships, was displayed at half mast to honor the sailors who died in the conflict.[22]

Within a few minutes of the commander's death, the *Minas Gerais* was under the control of its mutinous crew. Already, around 10:40 p.m., gunshots aboard the *Minas* were heard on other ships in the bay, and they replied by firing their own guns.[23] About that time, the leader of the revolt appeared, not having taken part in the previous violence. He was João Cândido Felisberto, a black man thirty years of age. The son of former slaves, João Cândido was a "big man of energy and resolution who had shown his grasp of the situation by ordering all the liquor on the *Minas Gerais* to be thrown overboard." These were the words of James Bryce, the British ambassador to the United States. The celebrated jurist happened to be in Rio at the moment of the revolt, gathering material for his book *South American Impressions*.[24]

Cândido, a seaman first class, had not participated in the initial violence, perhaps declining to do so to have greater moral authority, or perhaps using his hesitation to participate as a means of bargaining in his negotiations for the leadership of the movement.[25] According to the officer originally assigned to write the navy's official history, Oliveira Bello, Cândido was appointed leader by Francisco Dias Martins, a sailor on the *Bahia*.[26] Cândido chose Antônio Ferreira de Andrade as his secretary.[27] His first act was to announce the success of the insurrection on the *Minas* with two blasts of the 4.7-inch cannon; this was a signal to conspirators on other ships in the squadron. These blasts were answered by other rebel ships to show the success of their own mutinies.[28] In the city, onlookers were curious about—and some of them were frightened by—the cannon fire. They sought answers from military and naval personnel, but no one could tell them what was happening.[29]

The *São Paulo* was captained by Commander Pereira e Sousa, and some of the sailors aboard had witnessed the Republican revolution in Lisbon.[30] Seaman First Class Manuel Gregório de Nascimento informed the commander through Lieutenant Salustiano Lessa that the crew had rebelled. He asked Lessa and his fellow officers to quit the ship, except for the machinists. The rebel leader suggested that the officers take refuge on the *Duguay-Trouin*. All but one withdrew. Lt. Sales de Carvalho hid in the armory, but, apparently in despair, shot himself, later dying of his wounds.[31]

On the new destroyer of the Scout class, the *Bahia*, led by Commander Francisco de Matos, a twenty-year-old sailor named Francisco Dias Martins led the revolt.[32] First Lieutenant Mário Alves de Souza resisted the uprising on the ship, killing a rebel with his revolver; he was in turn dispatched by gunfire, despite the apparent intention of Dias Martins to avoid bloodshed.[33]

The other important vessel to join the rebellion was the older battleship *Deodoro*. An interlude of confusion and hesitation by the officers aboard that ship followed the mutineers' capture of the *Minas*, during which First Lieutenant João Paiva de Morais mistakenly thought the uprising was a rebellion to overthrow the government, a project he supported. But Paiva was drunk.[34] Corporal José Araújo then took command of the ship for the rebels. The mine-layer *República* and the torpedo gunboats *Tamoio* and *Timbira* also adhered to the revolt, expelling their officers.[35] The crew of the training ship *Benjamim* [sic] *Constant*, on which João Cândido and Gregório had once served, likewise induced their officers to leave without a struggle.[36] All the rebel ships displayed the red flag. Some of the men on the small vessels boarded the larger ones. Of the enlisted men in the squadron, almost half (2,379) had revolted, while 2,630 did not revolt, even if their fealty to the government might be suspect. Indeed, officers lacked confidence in the apparently loyal crews' allegiance, and the vast bulk of the firepower lay in the rebels' hands.[37] All but 2 percent of the rebel personnel were on four of the most powerful of the rebel-held ships—the *Minas*, the *São Paulo*, the *Bahia*, and the *Deodoro*.[38] One new vessel did not revolt—the *Rio Grande do Sul.* Though it had seamen aboard who supported the revolt, its officers maintained control. Nonetheless, it flew the red flag of rebellion, but only so as not to be destroyed by the two giant battleships.[39]

Beyond the line officers and men, there was a third class of naval personnel—the machinists and noncommissioned officers (*oficiais inferiores*, or NCOs). On the *São Paulo*, for example, none of these men left the ship. They were considered to be contracted technicians, whose job was to carry out auxiliary services; they were not combat officers, nor could they aspire to command posts.[40] Therefore, in Vice Admiral H. L. Martins's view, they tended toward neutrality in the struggle between officers and enlisted men.[41] One of them on the *Minas Gerais* even made common cause with the mutineers.[42] According to the historical sociologist Gilberto Freyre, these NCOs sometimes became the patrons and protectors of young sailors,[43] thereby bringing the two groups together in a way that might threaten the command structure. In addition, a total of eighteen British technicians were forcibly held aboard the two dreadnoughts.[44]

The two giant ships began to move at 1 a.m. on the 23rd, and the rebels requisitioned coal on the Ilha do Viana and seized barges carrying coal to other ships.[45] Aboard the *Minas Gerais*, the "admiral" of the fleet—João Cândido—who later referred to his assumed rank in quotation marks, issued orders and learned of the deaths on the *Bahia* at 2:15 a.m. An hour later he received word of the suicide of Lt. Sales de Carvalho on the *São Paulo*.[46] Around 5:00 a.m., the *Timbira*, now in government hands again, fired on the *Minas*. The latter returned fire with small caliber guns, driving back its attacker.[47] The *São Paulo* was positioned near the Ilha Fiscal, where the customs house was located, and the *Minas* was anchored in front of Praia Santa Luzia (Santa Luzia Beach); both had turned their bows toward the shore. The *Deodoro* and the *Bahia* drew between them.[48] The rebels informed two foreign ships—the *Duguay-Trouin* and the *Adamastor*—of the impending attacks on Brazilian targets.[49] At 7 a.m. on the 23rd, the *São Paulo* and the *Minas* moved toward the bar, and opened fire on the forts at Villegaignon and Santa Cruz.[50] The commanders of the

forts did not return fire, perhaps fearing destruction by the more powerful cannons of the dreadnoughts.[51] In any event, the government had instructed the commanders of the forts not to fire back.[52]

According to an account by an anonymous "Ex-sailor," Dias Martins
was responsible, at least in part, for conducting the movements of the
ships. In particular, he ordered Gregório not to put the *São Paulo* between
the Ilha Fiscal and the Ilha das Cobras, just offshore from the Naval Ministry, as Gregório had intended. Gregório's purpose was to choose a strategic location for attacking loyal ships, but Dias was afraid the huge ship
would run aground.[53] The battleships proceeded to pass through the bar
unscathed into the open sea. Beyond the bar, they would not be subject
to a surprise attack.

The rebel vessels returned at 7 a.m. on the 23rd, passing the Ilha das
Cobras "in good order," according to a competent observer, and firing on
the forts overlooking the city.[54] The battle plan was for the *São Paulo* to
attack the fortifications of the Cais Pharoux (the docks at the Praça XV
de Novembro,[55] near the Naval Ministry) and to eliminate all resistance
in the district of Glória, near the presidential palace; meanwhile, the
Deodoro would attack the forts of Santa Cruz and Gragoatá. The *Minas*
would attack those of São João and Imbuí.[56] Smaller ships were threatened by the crews of the dreadnoughts. A launch from the *São Paulo*
arrived at the training ship *Primeiro de Março* and informed the officers
that, if they didn't go ashore, the ship would be sunk. The officers complied. The rebel crews waved their caps at each other, and the band on the
São Paulo, like that on the *Minas Gerais*, was playing.[57]

The *Minas Gerais* fired its light guns on Niterói, the capital of Rio State,
across Guanabara Bay from the Federal Capital, around 8 a.m. At 9:45
Commander Neves's body, dispatched by the rebels on the *Minas* in a
launch, also arrived at the Naval Arsenal, on the Ilha das Cobras. The *São
Paulo* soon commenced firing at the island. At 11:55 a.m. the *Minas* discharged a "fortíssimo" blast toward Rio, apparently from a 12-inch gun.[58]

President Hermes in the meantime had come to the Naval Arsenal. He
only learned that morning that the crews of the *Deodoro*, the *República*,
and the *Timbira* had taken over their ships and joined the rebellion. A
shell from a rebel craft hit Castelo Hill not far from the downtown area
of Rio, and two, possibly three, civilians died.[59] The Naval Arsenal and
the naval bases on the Cobras and Villagaignon islands were hit, though
without great damage, perhaps because of the inexpert aim of the rebels.[60]

Other shots were fired by attackers and defenders later that day, as destroyers (*contra-torpedeiros*) approached the *São Paulo*. It fired at them around 2:30 p.m., and they retreated. That afternoon, the *Minas* even got off two blasts toward Catete, the presidential palace.[61] The rebels also lobbed shells into Niterói, across Guanabara Bay.

In the words of the naval historian of the revolt, "The most potent element of intimidation was the presence of those moving fortresses, [the *Minas Gerais* and the *São Paulo*], bristling with cannon, their powerful towers rotating menacingly, and moving about near the urban shoreline."[62] The widespread propaganda about the destructive power of the ships previously distributed by the government and its backers now served to spread terror among the citizenry.

What the rebels wanted was simple enough. But they issued demands in an apparently uncoordinated manner. Soon after the sailors took over the largest ships, the *Bahia* had radiogrammed Hermes: "We don't want the return of the lash. This we ask the president and the minister of the navy. We want an immediate answer. If we don't get it, we'll bombard the city and the ships that didn't revolt-[signed] the crews of the *Minas*, *São Paulo*, and *Bahia*."[63] A more formal set of demands was laid out in a neat handwritten declaration, probably composed days earlier. The document, a "memorial," addressed to the president of the republic stated:

> We, the sailors, Brazilian citizens and Republicans, no longer able to bear slavery in the Brazilian navy [and] the lack of protection that the Fatherland affords us, are rending the dark veil that covers the eyes of the patriotic and deceived people.
>
> Finding all the ships in our power . . . we [ask] Your Excellency to secure for Brazilian sailors the sacred rights that the laws of the Republic grant us . . . [including] removing incompetent and unworthy officers . . . ; reforming the immoral and shameful code that rules us, abolishing flogging, hand-paddling [*bolo*], and similar punishments; raising our pay, according to the latest plans of [Deputy] José Carlos de Carvalho;[64] educating the sailors who lack the ability to wear the uniform with pride; [and] putting into effect the work schedules that accompany [Carvalho's] program.
>
> Your Excellency has twelve (12) hours to send us a satisfactory reply, under the threat of seeing the Fatherland annihilated.
>
> Aboard the *São Paulo*, 22 November 1910.
>
> Note: The free movement of the messenger cannot be interrupted.
>
> The Sailors[65]

"Down with the lash" had not been a chance demand of disgruntled crewmen. The leading grievance that had provoked the revolt was the ancient and anachronistic practice of corporal punishment. On the night of November 21, the Bahian sailor Marcelino Rodrigues de Menezes had had to endure between 200 and 250 lashes on the *Minas Gerais*. His infraction was wounding Corporal Valdemar Rodrigues de Sousa with a razor ten days earlier.[66] Marcelino's flogging was the triggering event of the revolt.

Another complaint was the long and grueling workdays necessitated by serious understaffing of the great ships, topped off by required gymnastic exercises. On its first trip across the Atlantic, Commander Batista das Neves had reported to his superiors that the recently introduced regimen of gymnastics involved exercises of fifteen minutes in the morning and one hour (!) in the evening.[67] The fact that Sgt. Albuquerque, referred to above, was killed after being wounded, may be connected with the fact that he was director of the abhorrent gymnastics program.[68] The two Brazilian dreadnoughts were fully staffed with 106 officers and noncoms, and 887 men; at the time of the revolt, the *Minas* and the *São Paulo* had only about 350 men each.[69] Only half the stokers required for a full complement were available.[70] A third grievance was the poor quality of the food served to sailors,[71] a major factor in the celebrated *Potemkin* mutiny of 1905. And this problem was exacerbated by the fact that the British technicians aboard the dreadnoughts received special rations.[72] A fourth grievance was the meager pay the sailors received.[73] In an interview after the event one sailor (possibly Francisco Dias Martins) said that poor pay was a major reason for a conspiracy that preceded the revolt.[74] A final and less tangible demand, but nonetheless important, was that officers accord respect to the enlisted seamen. The sailors sent the "memorial" of their demands in another launch addressed to the president of the republic. Although it was the telegraph operator Ricardo de Freitas who had edited and possibly composed the message, Dias Martins was the sailor who directed that it be sent the government around 2 a.m.[75] In another message sent on the 23rd, the rebels said, "We don't want to harm anyone. We ask only for an increase in pay, and the end of scourging."[76]

Meanwhile, with shells falling on the city, the president and his cabinet had met during the early hours of November 23 to consider their options. One was to crush the rebellion. But if that were possible, it could only be done by destroying the great ships for which Brazil had paid such a dear price, blasting to oblivion Rio Branco's whole naval and diplomatic strategy for achieving regional power status for Brazil in the South Atlantic. Worse still, destroying the ships would leave Brazil defenseless against an attack by Argentina's new dreadnoughts, when they were completed in the latter months of 1911. Beyond those considerations was the sure wrath of Great Britain, if British subjects on board the battleships were to lose their lives. However, agreeing to an amnesty would have meant bowing to flagrant indiscipline in the navy, with the likely consequence of new and greater demands from the ranks in the future. Other evils attended this course of action: there would be a collapse of Brazil's prestige as a new player on the international stage, unforeseeable domestic political consequences for the humiliated government, including "political" revolts, and the probable rise in the cost of foreign credit to Brazil.[77] Worst of all, from the perspective of the officer class—an amnesty would imply the passive acceptance of the murder of several Brazilian officers, an offense that cried out for revenge.[78]

Hermes and his counselors realized that the Brazilian dreadnoughts, at that moment among the most powerful engines of destruction afloat, could use their 12-inch cannon aboard the two battleships to obliterate the shore batteries, including their modern 10-caliber howitzers. In addition, the rebels held the new cruiser *Bahia*, with ten 4.7-inch cannon, and six lesser ones; they also controlled the *Deodoro*, only a decade old and recently refitted. In terms of naval power, the government disposed of the antiquated cruiser *Barroso*, with 6-inch cannons and, of the new squadron, the new Scout *Rio Grande do Sul*, with ten 4.7-inch cannons, plus eight destroyers, and the torpedo boat *Goiás*.

The only feasible way to attack the rebels, thought Leal and his advisors, was to order the newly acquired destroyers to sink the great battleships under cover of darkness. But the torpedoes couldn't be fired without their firing caps, which were not yet in place. On the night of the revolt an officer was dispatched to get them on the Ilha de Boqueirão, only to learn that they were somewhere else! They had been stored on the little Ilhota do Paiol (Powder Magazine or Naval Armory), near Niterói, across the bay. But no one knew how to get the destroyers over there in the face of the rebel threat. Hours were lost. Another miscommunication followed, in which the vessel with the percussion caps failed to receive a radiogram telling its captain where to meet the torpedo-cruisers. Meanwhile a telegraph operator on the still-loyal ship *Paraíba*, Scipião Zanotti, passed word to the rebels that a destroyer attack was being planned, so the mutineers decided to spend the night of November 23–24 beyond the bar.[79]

Finally, on the morning of the 24th, the firing caps arrived. But to no effect, because they had not been designed for the new torpedoes. Only on the night of the 24th, forty-eight hours after the rebellion began, was the delivery of the proper firing caps accomplished. Even then, only in part: just twelve torpedoes were armed for the mission of the *Rio Grande do Sul.* If all that didn't produce utter consternation, it was then learned that the gyroscopes and the hydrostatic plates to assure the accuracy of the torpedoes had not been properly gauged.[80]

On the 23rd the government had also considered mining the bar, so that when the rebel squadron crossed the bar into the bay, the ships would be destroyed. But the requisite mines, like the percussion caps for the torpedoes, were stored in different locations around Guanabara Bay and were not numerous enough to carry out the project. Furthermore, mining the bay would also have risked antagonizing foreign governments, whose ships would have been endangered.[81] In fact, the British government was exercising strong pressure on its Brazilian counterpart not to destroy the rebel ships because of the British subjects working the engines of the dreadnoughts.[82]

The torpedoes were eventually fitted with their firing caps, and a plan of attack was finally agreed on, whereby the destroyers would position themselves near the bar inside the bay on the night of the 24th–25th. They would raise the red flag of rebellion, approach the rebel ships, and launch an assault when the dreadnoughts were crossing the line of the forts. At the same time government batteries would fire on the superstructures of the rebel ships, with the purpose of creating confusion among the crews.[83] Though the attack was otherwise well planned, it depended on surprise, and this was probably impossible to achieve because it involved issuing orders to loyal forces by radio. And radio operators on those ships were continually warning the rebels of government movements.[84] Given such information, leaders of the rebel ships chose to align themselves in a column, a formation that they knew would impede the use of artillery against them. But the admiralty was as ready as it could be to mount the attack.

On the night of the 22nd–23rd, the government had also decided to pursue a two-track strategy: although preparing for war, it would also parley with the mutineers.

While the admiralty had been constructing its military response, Congress, led by Senator Pinheiro Machado, had been seeking a peaceful solution, with the president's and Rio Branco's approval. In their "memorial," the rebels had mentioned their support for a bill raising seamen's salaries. It had been presented in Congress by Deputy José Carlos de Carvalho, a former naval officer and honorary commander who had been decorated for bravery during the Paraguayan War (1864–70) and had supported President Floriano against the revolt of 1893.[85] Carvalho was a member of the Riograndense congressional delegation, under the leadership of Senator Pinheiro Machado. On the night of November 22–23 at Catete Palace, Pinheiro, Hermes, and Naval Minister Leão decided that Carvalho was the best emissary to deal with the crisis, partly because the rebels had specifically mentioned him in connection with the bill to raise seamen's salaries. Upon being asked by Pinheiro on the morning of the 23rd to undertake the delicate mission of treating with the rebels, Deputy Carvalho donned his naval uniform. He boarded a launch from the Naval Arsenal and headed for the *Minas Gerais*.[86] He intercepted the "memorial" containing the sailors' grievances, while en route to the *Minas Gerais*. The rebels fired rifles at his small craft, so Carvalho was forced to board the *São Paulo*, where Gregório again explained the grievances of the men— barbaric corporal punishment, bad food,[87] and exhausting work schedules. Gregório also asked Carvalho to inspect the ship, showing him that the strongbox was being guarded by four armed men.

In addition, João Cândido sent to the *São Paulo* the sailor who had been so badly flogged, so that Carvalho could inspect his wounds. "The back of that sailor," Carvalho later reported to the Chamber of Deputies, "resembles a mullet slashed open for salting."[88] The president's envoy then went aboard the *Minas Gerais*, where he was received with military honors. João Cândido told him the rebels would end their revolt when their demands were met, if commanders to their liking were put aboard the battleships. Upon returning to shore, Carvalho met with the president and Senator Pinheiro Machado, and then he proceeded to the Chamber. He told his fellow deputies that when he asked the sailors of the *São Paulo* who accepted responsibility for the rebels' actions, they replied "all of us."[89] He laid out their grievances, as stated in the carefully handwritten "memorial." Carvalho also told the Chamber the ships "were maneuvering with precision." The ships still had machinists aboard and "were ready to go into action on the first signal from the head ship, the *Minas Gerais*. All the artillery was functioning well."[90] Encouraged by his reception in the Chamber of Deputies, at 4:30 p.m. on the 23rd Carvalho spoke with João Cândido again, offering a guarantee of amnesty to the sailors. According to Carvalho's account, Cândido, as leader of the movement, swore "as a [Brazilian] seaman" that he and his companions would not fire on the city if their demands were met.[91] At Catete Palace on the 24th, the president met with the minister of war, Dantas Barreto, the minister of the navy, Marques de Leão, and the minister of justice, Rivadávia Correia, a member of Pinheiro's Riograndense Republican Party. Carvalho and Pinheiro Machado were also present. The men debated whether an attack should still be attempted. Dantas believed the government could overcome the rebellion. But Carvalho heard Minister of the Navy Leão concede that, if the government resisted, it would cost many lives and "the loss of a large part of our military materiel." Pinheiro recommended reaching an understanding with the rebels and won over the president and his ministers.[92]

On the afternoon of November 23, the government sent an official note to the press, saying it would insist on the surrender of the rebels and would, if needed, torpedo the ships. Perhaps the government anticipated that the rebels would intercept the message, hoping that it would cow them into surrendering. In fact, the radio operator on the *Timbira*, a smaller ship, along with the operator on the *Tamoio* (whose crew had rebelled), picked up the information that the government was planning an attack with its loyal destroyers and passed it on. Consequently, the rebels decided to spend the night of the 23rd on the farther side of the bar, passing beyond the Marias, Redonda, and Cagarra Islands.[93]

At 10 a.m. on the 24th, João Cândido ordered that coal be brought to the *Bahia* and water to the *Deodoro*. According to one account, he insisted that the supplier of water take a drink first, to ensure that it wasn't poisoned.[94] At 2 p.m. that day Deputy Carvalho returned to the *Minas* to say that the government had decided to grant amnesty, according to João Cândido.[95] But that seems unlikely, since an amnesty had to be voted on by Congress. The matter came before the Senate the same day.

In the Senate debate on the 24th, Rui Barbosa, as leader of the opposition, agreed with the president of that body, Quintino Bocaiuva, that there was no "political" motive in the rebellion, and he assured the government that it could count on his support to maintain the law. Yet he demanded amnesty for the rebels. He argued that the men were cruelly overworked: "Ships constructed for crews of 900 men can't be manned, maintained, and repaired by 300 sailors."[96] The cannon placed on the *morros* of Rio could do little against "these invincible machines." Boarding parties, operating from launches would be useless; unfortunately, the dreadnoughts were "unconquerable." As for the sailors, Rui argued, despite their crime, they had revealed virtues that honor "our people and our race." They had thrown all the liquor overboard; they had posted guards for the strongboxes where the valuables were kept; they had put sentinels at the staterooms of the officers to keep them from being pilfered; they had been faithful to their idea of justice; and they had been loyal to each other. Rui had read the statements of Deputy José Carlos de Carvalho and noted that the sailors showed Carvalho the ships with pride, saying, in effect, "This is an honest revolt." "People of that sort are not to be despised," declared the senator from Bahia.[97] In the recent presidential campaign, Rui related, he had called for better wages and the suppression of corporal punishment. That inhumane institution had been abolished by the Provisional Government of the Republic, but the practice had returned, he implied, because of the demands of the officer corps. He made no mention of his own role in the process in 1890.[98]

There were other considerations: if the government didn't have the means to crush the movement, Rui asserted, then "it doesn't have the right to risk the destruction of the ships that represented a considerable part of the public assets of Brazil [and] precious resources for our defense."[99] He asked Pinheiro Machado: To maintain order, would you destroy this enormously expensive military equipment, the essential elements for the very existence of public order?[100] And the government did not have the right to destroy the thousands of men in the holds of those ships—"lives precious to us." Nor did it have the right to destroy "military resources difficult to assemble and prepare"; nor the right to permit the destruction of "the great Brazilian metropolis, with a million inhabitants, and all the riches it contains and the civilization it represents."[101]

Regarding the government's honor, Rui argued that amnesty was not the same as a pardon, which presupposes repentance, but a political act "by which one expunges [*faz esquecer*] the crime committed against public order."[102] On the issue of military honor, Rui observed that great generals, in the face of certain defeat, do not dishonor themselves by capitulating. Nor would it dishonor a levelheaded government to bow to necessity in a situation of which it was not a cause. Rui couldn't resist scoring a point about the militarism he had condemned in the presidential campaign. He stated that in the twenty years of the republic's existence, the armed forces had never been used to defend Brazil against foreign attack, but always to quell internal revolts. Following his peroration, Rui, together with the three senators from São Paulo whose political machine had backed his campaign for the presidency, presented the amnesty bill to the Senate.[103]

At that point José Gomes Pinheiro Machado, the leader of the majority in the Senate and its vice president, took the floor. Although Pinheiro was not a great orator, much less the intellectual that Rui was, he was an educated man and not an "extremely vulgar individual, without talent, without culture, without family traditions and prestige," as the social and literary critic Sílvio Romero would have it.[104]

Pinheiro Machado did not reveal his full hand from the beginning. He began his speech by saying:

> I make common cause with Your Excellency [Rui Barbosa] regarding the motives that generated such a grave and bizarre assault on the principles of discipline, which form the essential basis of the armed forces.
>
> We . . . have abundant proof that the insurrection is the product of indescribable, criminal abuses. Some are a flagrant violation of law, contrary to our better inclinations and the duties that [our] humanity demands, condemning the practice of humiliating punishments as disciplinary measures. These punishments degrade Man, depriving him of his self-respect and the basic conditions to do his duty . . .
>
> Though surprised by the uprising, all of us, recognizing the causes that generated it, are of course inclined to proclaim the justice of the protests that fostered it: Inadequate food, overwork, [and] corporal punishment, which are not in harmony with our liberal regime, with the law, nor with the present level of civilization and democratic culture we have attained.[105]

And yet, Pinheiro doubted that amnesty should be conceded in the face of "continuing acts of force, even if arising from grievances we all agree are just." A proclamation of amnesty might be the result of fear and concern for the great dangers that loom over the capital of the republic, he continued. But the

> revolt wasn't led by a responsible chieftain, nor directed by persons with the degree of culture sufficient to evaluate the damage they could cause, the evils that could result from bombardment of the capital, [including] the loss of precious lives. And I would further say, provoking the exodus of a population to save the lives of defenseless women and children, who don't have, as we do, the obligation to repel aggression, if it comes.
>
> My spirit vacillates, therefore, in trying to discover wherein lies the greater evil: in immediately granting the measures urged by the rebels and passing

over their misdeeds . . . given the dangers I confess are real, [or, in trying to overwhelm the rebels]. Therefore I have told the illustrious Senator from Bahia I don't oppose the essence of the idea he presented, because I agree with him, but I have doubts about whether such a measure is opportune.[106]

Rui had agreed to Deputy Carvalho's talks with the rebels, Pinheiro went on. The sailors could demand still more: "We could be making successive concessions that would result in undermining the authority of the *pátria* itself."[107] Rui reminds us, said Pinheiro, that our weapons have been used to arm seditions. But "I would remind His Excellency that powerful armaments don't produce revolutions; rather, [the cause is] indiscipline and anarchy among the social classes."[108]

> What is happening at this moment is a unique situation in the history of humanity: two warships, the most modern and powerful in the world, which evidently place the rest of the navy in a situation of great inferiority, . . . exercise a dominion without parallel, an unquestionable supremacy in the waters of this capital city. . . .
>
> But my conviction [is] that to keep the [peace], it is essential that we be strong in order to be respected; [and] that we must conserve these precious instruments, designed only to repel any affronts that could be directed against us.[109]

Pinheiro pointed out that if public order were violated and remained unpunished, other malcontents would be able to rise up against the government. Such a situation could lead to even greater concessions by the government, resulting in utter dishonor.[110]

Rui Barbosa then objected that Brazil found itself in a civil war, in which the government could only concede amnesty to save the great ships. There was no dishonor in this course of action.[111] Pinheiro retorted:

> In the first place it isn't proven that that movement can't be overcome; on the contrary, I am convinced that it will inevitably be conquered, after having produced great evils, it is true. And I ought to inform the noble Senator that at this moment our emissaries are negotiating amnesty with the rebels . . . [an amnesty] that in my opinion should only be conceded after the rebels lay down their arms, submitting to the legitimate authorities. I must add that everything makes me believe that the conditions proposed by our emissaries will not be spurned.[112]

But Rui Barbosa wasn't satisfied: the sailors know their lives might be sacrificed if they surrendered. Even if they couldn't prolong the fight for months, they had enough firepower to destroy the capital of the republic, a situation that would produce the "annihilation of the present government." Rui didn't understand why, if Pinheiro had agreed to the amnesty offered to the rebels by Deputy Carvalho, he wouldn't accept immediate amnesty. Pinheiro Machado replied that amnesty had been accepted by other senators and deputies, but it was conditional on the rebels' surrendering their arms.[113]

About that time Pinheiro learned by telephone that the rebels had radioed the president that they repented their actions, and that they would lay down their arms in the expectation that Congress would grant an amnesty. After a dramatic pause, the senator from Rio Grande do Sul declared:

> Mr. President, I have the [good] fortune at this moment to communicate to you and the Senate the gratifying news that the mediation of Deputy José Carlos de Carvalho—as the emissary of the men with indisputable responsibilities in this government—has been crowned with success. The rebels have just informed the President of the Republic that they submit to legal authority, asking for amnesty in exchange. . . . Consequently, the objections I made [earlier] can be dispensed with. . . . We may therefore vote for the bill, without the shadow of terror [over us], certain that we are deliberating freely, now that the revolt has ended.[114]

But did the rebels really send that message, repenting their actions and asking for clemency? One authority thinks it was invented by Deputy Carvalho, to save face for Congress and the executive. In any event, it may have been rewritten by Carvalho to get the optimum effect in Congress.[115] Whether Pinheiro Machado knew or suspected the message to be of dubious authenticity, it allowed him to side with those who would save the ships. Rui's amnesty bill was then read and sanctioned unanimously on the evening of November 24. It seems likely that Rui Barbosa had played the role in the debate that Pinheiro Machado had designed for him—to show why the government had to grant amnesty, while Pinheiro demonstrated that it could be done on face-saving terms for the government.

Carvalho had undertaken a third mission to the sailors on the 24th, appealing to their patriotism and concern for the lives of those in the city. During his trip, he received a radiogram that the Senate had voted unanimously for an amnesty, but the Chamber had yet to vote. The atmosphere was still tense, and when Carvalho withdrew from the *Minas Gerais*, he was accompanied by the ship's Italian band. They argued (conveniently) that their contract had expired.[116]

Beyond the preparations for war and the peace-seeking intervention of Congress, Foreign Minister Rio Branco undertook a third initiative, probably without the president's knowledge, that might convince Hermes of the wisdom of granting an amnesty. On the afternoon of the 24th, he intervened personally in the crisis, in effect bypassing the president of the republic and the minister of the navy. The baron deputized his close friend, Lieutenant-Commander Jorge Dodsworth Martins, to intercede. He would contact the leader of the planned attack, Commander Filinto Perry,[117] whom João Cândido had once served on the training ship *Primeiro de Março*.[118] Dodsworth and Rio Branco lunched at the latter's favorite restaurant, the Brahma, where the baron made a persuasive appeal. When it was relayed to them, Rio Branco's reasoning seems also to have convinced the minister of the navy and the president of the republic. It was this: even the most powerful navy in the world, that of Great Britain, at one time had encountered similar problems and had overcome them. Rio Branco cited an incident in Britain's struggle against the French revolutionaries in 1797. The rebellion at Spithead in April of that year had forced William Pitt the Younger to yield, when the crews of sixteen ships of the Channel fleet had mutinied. Their remonstrances concerned working conditions and pay, and they had put ashore several officers they considered excessive disciplinarians. The government, locked in a bitter struggle with France, granted a pardon. But the following month another mutiny at the Nore (an anchorage in the Thames) raised the stakes, with demands for changes in the Articles of War and other concessions. The mutineers tried to blockade the Thames, but the government now resolved to suppress the mutiny with severity. The rebellion fell apart, and the leading mutineers were hanged, while others were flogged.[119]

Rio Branco argued that history had forgotten the initial humiliation of the British government. In the case of Brazil, in the words of his luncheon guest, Dodsworth Martins, the foreign minister believed the two dreadnoughts "represented South American naval equilibrium, a position we couldn't lose at any price."[120] Rio Branco probably assumed that a second rebellion would follow in Brazil, as it had in Britain, with a result similar to that of the British case. Perhaps he left that outcome for President Hermes and Naval Minister Leão to infer.

Furthermore, there were outside political pressures to settle the matter quickly. The British embassy reported that its minister "has protested in the name of his government against any idea of torpedoing the mutinous warships in view of the fact that there are British subjects on board. The Fourth Cruiser Squadron [under Admiral Farquhar], now at Montevideo, has received orders to proceed at once to Rio de Janeiro."[121] Would the United States make a similar display of power? In the naval crisis of 1893 the United States had played a decisive role, when rebel ships had tried to blockade Guanabara Bay to overthrow the government of Floriano Peixoto.[122] Now, the American ambassador to Brazil, no doubt conscious of the importance of a US showing on this occasion, had inquired whether his government could dispatch a warship. The US envoy was informed that the nearest available vessel was at Hampton Roads, Virginia, and that preparation and steaming time would amount to seventeen to twenty days—too long a period to affect the outcome of the crisis.[123]

Cariocas were well aware of the recent bombing of Manaus, the state capital of Amazonas, by the military. Older residents of Rio would recall the revolt of the squadron against President Floriano, exactly seventeen years earlier, when the city had been bombed by Admiral Custódio de Melo. Hermes had in fact initially thought the rebellion might be led by an admiral, Alexandre de Alencar, who had commanded the great ship *Aquidabã* in the earlier conflict. In addition, the government had to be concerned about foreign intervention, a major affront to Brazilian sovereignty in 1893. Finally, Cariocas who remembered the 1893 revolt doubtless feared a repetition of the bombings of that time, when thousands of people fled Niterói and Rio.

When the Hermes government now announced that it would attack the rebel-held ships, some three thousand of Rio's wealthier citizens, aware of the devastating power of the two great warships and fearing more shelling of the capital city, fled the Federal District for the summer capital Petrópolis. Other rich people escaped in their cars to Tijuca Forest. Many less opulent Cariocas headed for Rio's suburbs.[124] Trains leaving the national capital were packed. According to the weekly magazine *O Malho*, "Only those who witness[ed] the panic . . . can imagine what terror there was." People took bedding, kitchen utensils, suitcases, dogs, cats, and parrots with them. The government's initial defiance of the rebels may have been a bluff, a trial balloon that produced an unanticipated result.[125]

While Cariocas were panicking, the government proceeded with its long-delayed plan of attack. At 2 a.m. on the 25th, the minister of the navy was told to act. Leão had prepared a document stating, "The minister of the navy . . . orders the commander of [name of ship] to attack the rebel-held ships with the utmost energy, sinking them, without considering the sacrifice. The least hesitation will be [treated as] a criminal act."[126] But at 3 a.m. the assault was temporarily halted, as Senator Pinheiro Machado and Deputy Carvalho endeavored to bring about a congressional amnesty.

On the 25th a radiogram from the *Minas Gerais* was directed not to the minister of the navy, but—impudently—to the Brazilian people and president of the republic, in that order. "The sailors of the *Minas Gerais*, the *São Paulo*, the *Bahia*, and the *Deodoro*, as well as other warships displaying the red flag, have no other aim than securing the abolition of the infamous lash that debases the citizen and the moral qualities of our armed forces." We have repeatedly asked for this, they said, and, in addition, the insurgents demanded the end of the excessive work routines and "the absolute lack of consideration with which we were always treated." All this was a restatement of the central points of the handwritten "memorial." Repeating their demand for the "complete abolition of corporal punishment," the seamen regretted that the uprising had occurred in the beginning of Marshal Hermes's presidency, and they appealed to the Brazilian people for sympathy for their cause. They added that the rebels would act in their own defense if attacked. The message was signed, not by a rebel leader, but by "the Sailors of the Brazilian Fleet."[127]

From the *São Paulo*, also on the 25th, came a message that the revolted crews would accept "peace terms" if the president of the republic came in person to the ships, with a committee of senators and deputies, and decree that (1) corporal punishment be abolished in the navy, (2) officers and non-commissioned officers be prohibited from verbally abusing the sailors, and (3) an amnesty be declared for the rebels. They repeated the demand for the abolition of flogging "and other barbarous punishments. [We do this] because of our right to liberty, so that the Brazilian navy may become a fleet of citizens and not a plantation of slaves whose only right is to be whipped by their masters." The sailors closed their message with a mixture of submission and bold assertion: "In the name of the Brazilian navy, we are your humble subordinates. Health and Fraternity. The sailors in revolt."[128]

The rebels continued to communicate with the government and directed another message to Hermes on the 25th, altering their tone. As the "petitioners" (*reclamantes*) now, they returned to their claim to the rights of citizens. Those at fault, they alleged, were "the officers who make us their slaves." The revolt wasn't a matter "of politics, but rather of the rights of the miserable sailors." They appealed to the president to resolve the problem.[129] Following the Senate's lead, the Chamber of Deputies overwhelmingly approved the amnesty bill on November 25, and Hermes signed it around 5 p.m. The naval plan for a full-scale attack was now finally scrubbed.[130]

Deputy Carvalho immediately radioed the text to the *Minas Gerais.* Carvalho received a message from the *São Paulo*: "If there is any deception, you will suffer the consequences. We are ready to sell our lives at a high price." The radiogram was signed "the revolted sailors" (*os revoltosos*), not the term they had recently used, "the petitioners."[131] They also wanted a committee of officers to come aboard the ships, possibly to be used as hostages.[132] The government wisely refused to send any such committee.

On his fourth and final mission at 7 p.m. on November 25, Carvalho explained the amnesty to the sailors. João Cândido, in consultation with other leaders, agreed to the terms, although there may have been dissent among sailors on the *Deodoro*.[133] And possibly for a good reason: small craft had attacked the *Deodoro* in the early morning hours of the 25th, heightening the rebels' suspicions of trickery.[134] The strike may have been a probe to learn whether they could be surprised. But radio operators aboard the rebel ships had warned the sailors of the attack at the time when Carvalho was parleying with them, and he felt betrayed by the government for not advising him of any attack. He contacted Pinheiro Machado, who assured him everything was under control. It may be that the naval assault was canceled at that moment. In any event, the rebels chased off their assailants on the smaller boats with a few shots. Earlier, they had been informed by the *Paraíba's* telegrapher, Scipião Zanotti, that the government's attack had been canceled. Carvalho then toiled successfully to assure the revolted sailors of the government's sincerity.[135]

The rebels had entered the bay around 1 p.m. on the 25th and retired beyond the bar at 10 p.m. They discharged their twelve-inch cannons in celebration. Such noise went on through the night, and the mutineers made a triumphal reentry on the 26th. But they were still leery: they decided to enter the bay in a column, with the *Bahia* in the lead. If it were attacked, the rebels planned to open fire on the city.[136] At 7:30 a.m. the *São Paulo* and the *Bahia* crossed the bar into Guanabara Bay. Only at 2 p.m. did the *Minas Gerais* and *Deodoro* arrive, both still displaying the red flag. At 3:30 p.m. Commander João Pereira Leite, designated by the rebel seamen to assume control of the *Minas Gerais*, received full honors and took command of the lead ship.[137] But, according to Cândido, he told the sailors that the government wanted them to disembark on Villa-gaignon Island. The crews objected, perhaps fearing immediate capture, and Pereira Leite went back ashore to discuss the matter with the government. He returned to the ship and reassumed command at 7:35 p.m.[138] The other ships were also returned to high-ranking officers.[139]

War Minister Dantas, though conceding that Hermes had remained calm throughout the crisis, viewed the president's action as giving in to Rio Branco and Pinheiro Machado.[140] At all events, there was no satisfactory way for President Hermes to save face, but Senator Antônio Azeredo of Mato Grosso, one of Pinheiro's henchmen, did his best in a speech before the Senate on November 28. He pointed to instances in the stolid marshal-president's career that had demonstrated his personal bravery. "Conscious of his obligations, His Excellency had been ready to resist the revolt of the sailors, and was certain that the government would prevail. This, because the resources the rebels disposed of would be destroyed within a few days, and the Government would triumph." Yet Hermes did his duty, continued Azevedo, ceding because of the raison d'état that resulted in an amnesty.[141] Meanwhile, the Senate approved a resolution for the construction of a sarcophagus for the remains of João Batista das Neves, commander of the *Minas Gerais*.

Figure 1. Praça Quinze de Novembro, next to the Ministry of the Navy. Source: Biblioteca Nacional.

Figure 2. Commander Batista das Neves and the *Minas Gerais*. Source: Biblioteca Nacional.

Figure 3. Brazilian sailors control the dreadnoughts. Source: Biblioteca Nacional.

Figure 4. João Cândido and his secretary. Source: Museu da Imagem e do Som.

Figure 5. Manuel Gregório do Nascimento, "commander" of the *São Paulo*. Source: Biblioteca Nacional.

Figure 6. André Avelino and Manuel Gregório de Nascimento on the *São Paulo*.
Source: Museu da Imagem e do Som.

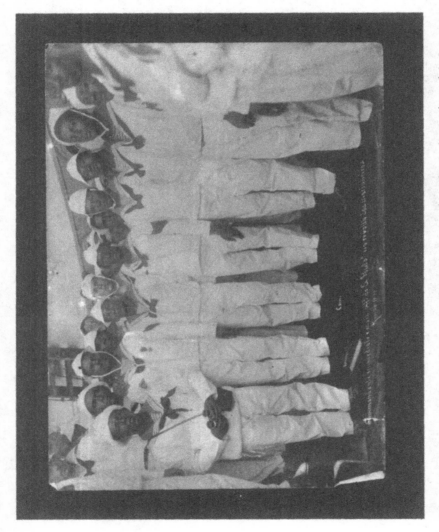

Figure 7. Sailors on the *São Paulo* (Gregório do Nascimento with André Avelino to his right). Source: Museu da Imagem e do Som.

Figure 8. Rebel sailors on the *Bahia* (Dias Martins with banner around neck). Source: Asociação Brasileira de Imprensa.

Figure 9. Rebel crews aboard the *Minas Gerais*. Source: Museu da Imagem e do Som.

Figure 10. Rebel crews aboard the *São Paulo*, with Sugarloaf Mountain in the background. Source: Museu da Imagem e do Som.

Figure 11. Mutinous sailors on the *São Paulo* demand liberty. Source: Biblioteca Nacional.

Figure 12. João Cândido reading the text of the amnesty decree (detail of Figure 4). Source: Biblioteca Nacional.

Figure 13. Commander Pereira Leite assuming control of the *Minas Gerais.* Source: Biblioteca Nacional.

Figure 14. "The discipline of the future." Source: Asociação Brasileira de Imprensa.

Figure 15. Hermes suppresses the second revolt. Source: Biblioteca Nacional.

O chefe da esquadra rebelde sahindo escoltado do Hospital Central do Exercito.

Figure 16. João Cândido being led to prison. Source: Biblioteca Nacional.

Figure 17. João Cândido as a prisoner. Source: Biblioteca Nacional.

Figure 18. José Gomes Pinheiro Machado on horseback. Source: Artur Ferreira Filho.

§3 The Rebels and Their Motives

The government took the position from the start that the goal of the revolt had not been "political"—a claim that was repeated again and again in the next few days, in Brazil and abroad; rather, said the spokesmen for the Hermes administration, the dispute had been about work rules. In fact, it was about both. Brazil was the last country in the Western world where flogging was still permitted in its navy. Corporal punishment had been a universal form of discipline in Western navies through the Napoleonic era. But whipping had been abolished in Spain in 1823, in France in 1860, in the United States in 1862, in newly united Germany in 1872, in Britain in 1881, in Portugal in 1895, and even in Tsarist Russia—a country infamous for the application of the knout—in 1904.

Brazil's Republican constitution of 1891 had confirmed the provisions of its imperial predecessor of 1824, abolishing flogging as a form of torture. Whipping was permitted, however, in the imperial military and naval codes,[1] though such punishment was terminated in the army in 1874. The 1891 constitution overlooked the fact that in the previous year Rui Barbosa, finance minister in the provisional government of Deodoro da Fonseca, had created a loophole for corporal punishment. On April 12, 1890, Rui, the paladin of liberalism who would soon be the principal author of the new constitution, had created a set of naval regulations called the Companhia Correcional. Cosigned by Minister of the Navy Eduardo Wandenkolk, probably the instigator of this measure, Rui's regulations permitted up to twenty-five lashes per day. But an increase in the number of strokes was left to the "prudent discretion of the [ship's] commander."[2] Thus whipping continued after the new constitution had theoretically outlawed it.

Flogging was dreaded enough that sailors would sometimes have the crucifixion tattooed on their backs, in the hope of averting or mitigating the application of the lash. The punishment also involved public humiliation before one's peers, as the men were required to muster for the ceremony. In the minds of the seamen, some of whose parents were born slaves, the lash was intimately associated with the slave regime and was therefore probably even more intolerable than it would have been in navies where there was no such association.[3] Although the punishment was sometimes administered while the victim was wearing a shirt, the whipping of Marcelino Rodrigues—who had received eight to ten times the daily limit of twenty-five lashes—could only be considered an outrage. In fact, his wounds were grievous, as Deputy Carvalho, an eyewitness, had reported to Congress. Naval officers contended that the threat of whipping was an essential element in maintaining discipline aboard ship.[4] Moreover, some even believed flogging gave sailors the opportunity to demonstrate their "physical and moral superiority," to their peers by showing how well they could "take it."[5]

Given this paramount grievance, when and where was the revolt planned? João Cândido, in his interview with the journalist Hélio Silva in 1968, said plotting for the revolt began in 1908 and continued in Britain during the seamen's training for operating the dreadnoughts. But in Cândido's "Memories" of 1912–13, probably a more reliable source because of its much earlier appearance, he only mentions three specific dates in September and October 1910, when plotting took place. Cândido implies that he was present, though this is disputed by another source. An interview with "one of the leaders" (possibly Francisco Dias Martins) in the *Diário de Notícias*, a week after the first revolt broke out, traces the plotting to the arrival of the *Bahia* in Buenos Aires in October 1910, following the ship's voyage to Chile. But the anonymous "Ex-sailor," in 1948, possibly the same Dias Martins, only mentions such conspiracies occurring in Rio in 1910.[6] Of course, planning a revolt may begin with speculation or "loose talk," so the allegations may not be irreconcilable. In any event, there can be little doubt that the revolt was conceived of and carried off brilliantly. Vice Admiral H. L. Martins, the navy's authority on the subject and one with no reason to laud the rebels, believed "the revolt was really well planned, well coordinated (except the massacre on the *Minas Gerais*), and rigorously kept secret."[7] The execution of the plot was postponed several times. According to "Ex-sailor," Manuel Gregório Nascimento, the future rebel commander of the *São Paulo*, had wanted the rebellion to occur when the new president came aboard the great battleships as part of the naval review connected with the inaugural ceremonies. However, Dias Martins, who had been in Buenos Aires at the time of the inauguration of Argentine President Roque Sáenz Peña on October 1, 1910, argued that such timing would make the movement appear to be a "political" rebellion against a particular president, as opposed to a demand for the rights of the sailors.[8] He won over his fellow conspirators.

Who were the leaders of a revolt that had allowed common sailors to wrest control of the bulk of the squadron's firepower? Chief among them and overall commander was Seaman First Class João Cândido Felisberto, whose official name in the navy was simply "João Cândido." (Because an officer in the Brazilian navy had precisely the same name, João Cândido was not allowed to use the surname Felisberto.)

On November 22 he became de facto captain of the *Minas Gerais*, the ship where the revolt had begun and the one that had signaled the other vessels that the movement was successfully underway. He was also commander of the whole rebel squadron, whose crews included nearly twenty-four hundred men. His assigned role in the navy was that of helmsman, whose duty it was to guide a ship in and out of harbors. This was a critical skill for the success of the revolt because the rebel ships had to be led out of range of the shore batteries and beyond the bar, where they would not be surprised by a nighttime naval attack by the government. He was probably the best helmsman among the rebels, even in the unsympathetic view of his fellow rebel "Ex-sailor."[9] According to the journalist Edmar Morel, who wrote the first full account of the revolt, João Cândido was the first common sailor anywhere ever to command a squadron. Not quite: yet he was probably the first helmsman to control a whole squadron since Alcibiades had given Antiochus charge of the Athenian fleet in 406 BCE during the Peloppenisian War.[10]

A powerfully built black man with high cheekbones and a bristling moustache, João Cândido was thirty years old in 1910. He had been born the son of slaves, or recently manumitted slaves, on a cattle ranch in Rio Grande do Sul.[11] He hailed from the county of Rio Pardo. But Rio Pardo was not just any small community in Rio Grande do Sul. It was the location of an important military school, as well as the residence of military officers on the way up the command structure. It was also the birthplace of Alexandrino de Alencar, the minister of the navy who had planned the naval expansion of 1906 and had just completed his term of office in November 1910.[12] The owner of the ranch on which João Cândido was born, João Felipe Correia, was a friend of Alencar, and João Cândido considered himself Alencar's client.[13] In addition, the black sailor was befriended by another *gaúcho*, Pinheiro Machado, who in later years João Cândido believed had saved his life.[14] In a society still bound together by patronage and favor, such connections were often crucial. Whether they played a role in the events at issue is debatable, but the likelihood that some of the other sailors knew about João Cândido's relationships, especially that with Alencar, probably aided Cândido in gaining the leadership of the revolt.

The black sailor from Rio Grande had begun his naval career at the School for Naval Apprentices in Porto Alegre, the state capital. He had entered the school in 1895, and in his fifteen years' service, João Cândido had held a number of posts and had made many long voyages. Early in his career Cândido had been topman, like Melville's Billy Budd, with responsibility for the main mast. He had also been a signalman.[15] João Cândido was a member of the generation of sailors who made the transition from sailing vessels to steam-powered ironclads. Cândido himself had never been flogged, but he was put into solitary confinement several times over the years for brawls with, or attacks on, other sailors.[16] In 1909 and 1910, however, he was also twice cited for exemplary conduct. Cândido was promoted to corporal (*cabo*) in 1903, but was demoted to seaman first-class two years later, for having brought liquor aboard his ship.[17] He had traveled through the Amazon Valley in 1903 and 1904 during the Bolivian crisis, in which Foreign Minister Rio Branco used naval power to bring Acre under Brazilian control.[18] Subsequently, João Cândido sailed to Montevideo, Buenos Aires, and up the Rio de la Plata estuary to Asunción, the capital of Paraguay. He reenlisted in 1905, sailed to Europe, and stepped ashore at Christiana (Oslo, after 1924), Stockholm, Wilhelmshaven, Amsterdam, Le Havre, Cherbourg, Lisbon, and Las Palmas (Canary Islands). By his own account in 1913, on that voyage Cândido had also stopped at Kronstadt, the fortress town protecting St. Petersburg, though this port does not appear in his official record. The detail is potentially significant, in that he could have learned of the Potemkin rebellion in Odessa at that time. Cândido returned to Rio in December 1906. It was on this trip, apparently, that he saw the Kaiser reviewing the German squadron at the Kiel Canal.[19]

From January to March 1907, João Cândido was engaged in exercises in torpedoing, artillery, piloting (*evoluções*), and assisting in hydrographic surveys on the Brazilian coast south of the federal capital. In March 1909, he joined the crew of the *Riachuelo*, when it took former President Campos Sales to Buenos Aires, where he would serve as ambassador. But Cândido spent most of his time in 1909 on the training ship *Benjamim Constant*.[20] He was chosen to participate in training in England for the operation of the *Minas Gerais* and arrived in Plymouth in August 1909, continuing on a month later to Newcastle-upon-Tyne. There he spent forty days training to act as helmsman for the battleship.[21] Cândido sailed for Lisbon at the end of October, and after visiting Toulon and Dieppe by way of Paris, he returned to Newcastle at the end of November for further instruction. Also in 1909 and 1910, on different ships, he was chosen by his fellow sailors to play Neptune in the festivities on crossing the equator.[22] This was an indication of his prestige among fellow sailors. Cândido commanded respect partly because he was tall and powerful, and he was old enough to enjoy prestige among the generation of sailors, who, like himself, had been trained on wind-powered vessels. Many of these older seamen did not adapt well to the continuous tasks of maintenance required by modern steam-powered battleships. The older men were known as "gorgotas" and "conegaços"—terms signifying "veteran sailors."[23] Among the more youthful men, Cândido was favored by the organizers of the plot.[24]

Other leaders of the rebellion were considerably younger than João Cândido, remarkably young for the roles they played. They ranged in age from twenty to twenty-three, but this is more readily understandable when one takes into account that the majority of the men in the ranks were between seventeen and twenty-two years old.[25] This situation is perhaps surprising since terms of service were lengthy, but high rates of desertion largely explain the difference.

Two of the young leaders stood out: they were Manuel Gregório de Nascimento and Francisco Dias Martins.[26] Unlike João Cândido, these sailors had participated in the detailed planning of the rebellion, and their voices were important in the decision to entrust the overall leadership to Cândido.[27] The naval historian Bello, who calls Cândido a *preto* (black) considers Gregório a *caboclo* (man of Indian, black, and white ancestry).[28] Dias Martins may have been white, though the evidence is far from conclusive. Gregório had been born in the Northeastern state of Alagoas, and he was twenty-two or twenty-three at the time of the revolt. In the navy he had been a musician, but later studied torpedoing and artillery, and then was given responsibility for the sailors' mess.[29] He had traveled around the Mediterranean in 1904 and was cited by the president of the republic for exemplary discipline. The Alagoan sailor was aboard a ship that toured northern Europe in 1906, the training ship *Benjamim Constant*, on which João Cândido was also a crewman.[30] Two years later Gregório sailed around the world on that ship, passing from Montevideo to Valparaíso and Callao. The vessel proceeded across the Pacific to Honolulu, Yokohama, Shanghai, Singapore, Colombo, Aden, Naples, and Toulon (where it had been built), among other ports. Gregório returned to Rio de Janeiro in December 1908. A seaman first-class since 1907, he was twice again cited for exemplary conduct, despite having spent four days in solitary confinement for a run-in with another sailor.[31]

At age twenty, Francisco Dias Martins was one of the two youngest of the leaders of the revolt.[32] He was one of the ideologues and probably the leading tactician of the complex operation. Dias was also the best schooled of the group. "Ex-sailor" asserts that Dias Martins had received a complete secondary education and descended from a prestigious family in Ceará,[33] in marked contrast with the "poor and ignorant" João Cândido. "Ex-sailor" surely exaggerates on both matters, because Dias Martins's mother was described in the *Gazeta de Notícias* in 1912 as "very poor,"[34] and João Cândido could read. Born in Ceará, Dias Martins joined the navy in 1906 and was sent to the School of Naval Apprentices in his home state in 1907. He became seaman first-class the same year. Dias was put in the brig early in 1908 for having beaten another sailor. He was cited for good conduct in a presidential decree that July, but was put in the stocks once for making insulting remarks to an officer. Dias Martins was sent to Newcastle from Rio to join the crew of the new scout *Bahia* in February 1910. He left Newcastle on the ship in April, bound for Rio, with a specialty in engines (*machinas em movimento*). He became guardian of the armory of the *Bahia*, and in that capacity he traveled from Rio to Valparaíso in September, when the Brazilian government sent the ship to Chile to participate in that country's centennial celebration. The *Bahia* was also present at the inauguration of the Argentine president in Buenos Aires, in October 1910. The young sailor returned to Rio the same month.[35]

Dias Martins was one of the most articulate members of the rebels, but the naval historian H. L. Martins believes he did not write the manifesto. Rather, it was Ricardo Freitas, a telegraph operator, who also had been one of the men sent to England for instruction in handling the dreadnoughts.[36] But Dias apparently did dominate the discussions held on November 13 about when to launch the revolt. He convinced his fellow plotters not to revolt on November 15, the day of Hermes's inauguration, since such action might be seen as having been motivated by the president's political enemies. Years later, Marcelino Rodrigues, the sailor whose savage flogging had touched off the rebellion, gave Dias the credit for initiating the plot to revolt during the *Bahia*'s trip to Chile earlier in 1910, although he credited João Cândido with the leadership of the movement once the revolt had begun.[37]

An anonymous letter to a high-ranking naval official adds important details, and the author was probably Dias Martins himself. In the letter written in 1948 by "Ex-sailor" the author makes Dias the undisputed organizer of the uprising—"the intellectual, moral and real leader of the revolt." The writer even calls Cândido a lickspittle of the officers, "capable of cleaning the soles of their shoes with his tongue." (The only evidence for this judgment seems to be that Cândido, after the amnesty, reported on the men who were flaunting discipline on his ship.) "What he had over than the other helmsmen," wrote the anonymous former sailor, "was his practiced exit and entry from the bar in Rio." Some other allegations in the narrative are false, such as the assertion that Deputy José Carlos Carvalho could only go onto the other ships after negotiating with Dias Martins on the *Bahia*.[38] Rather, Carvalho went straight to the *São Paulo*, to avoid hostile gunfire, spoke with Gregório, and then proceeded to deal with João Cândido on the *Minas Gerais*.

Naval officers, both contemporaries and later writers—with the honorable exception of H. L. Martins—see the letter of "Ex-sailor" as evidence that Dias Martins led the rebellion in every sense.[39] Their subtext seems to be that Dias Martins was white, as opposed to what "Ex-sailor" called the "Negro" João Cândido.[40] But *was* Dias Martins white? The only photo I have found shows him on the *Bahia* along with many other sailors, all of whose "race" is difficult to determine, but he might have been less African in appearance.[41] Moreover, the out-of-focus photograph of his mother and sister on the first page of the *Gazeta de Notícias* on December 31, 1912, seem to depict two women of mixed race. This is all the more likely, given that they were poor and came from the interior of Ceará. Moreover, according to naval records, Dias was illegitimate,[42] as was the case for the vast majority of the sailors, despite "Ex-sailor's" claim that the young man was a "descendant of a rich and prestigious family of Ceará." In sum, on the matter of race, little more could be safely said other than that Dias Martins was probably less African in appearance than João Cândido.

The navy did attempt to compile detailed records about race and other physical and legal characteristics of its personnel. In January 1908 the new Bureau of Naval Identification (Gabinete de Identificação d'Armada) began to classify all officers and men in this manner. The bureau's objective was to compile dossiers on the sailors' parents (if known; many were orphans), state of birth, age, height, race, hair (kinky, curly, or straight), facial features, scars and tattoos, level of education, and civil status. On rare occasions, photos and fingerprints were provided as well. A similar project by the police of Rio de Janeiro was underway for criminal suspects. These undertakings were probably inspired by the positivist criminology of the Italian sociologist Cesare Lombroso, whose work was then widely admired in the Mediterranean world.

During 1908 the navy collected detailed files on 1,285 men, out of the 3,274 on active duty, according to Naval Minister Alencar.[43] In 1909, 904 files were created, but there was some overlap with the 1908 figures. In 1910 and 1911 the project continued, but only to exclude suspected rebels or sympathizers from naval service.[44] Thus no systematic and complete sets of data were obtained for any single year. Of the 1908 materials—the most extensive—few names appear of those who participated in the revolt of November 1910. Were the files of the rebel leaders removed for any reason?[45] Or were their dossiers purposely destroyed? It seems most likely that the rebel leaders were simply never classified.[46] None of the leaders of the rebellion appear among the sailors' names recorded for 1908, but a few of those who participated in the revolt of November *were* listed. Among them was Aristides Pereira da Silva, known as "Chaminé," the sailor who had urinated on the corpse of Commander Batista Neves. In 1910 he was twenty years old, a native of Minas Gerais of known parents. His level of instruction was recorded as "none," and he was relatively tall (1.75 meters, or 5 feet 9 inches). He was classified as black (*preto*) with thick lips, and beardless. His hair was "unruly." He was to have a short life. Another rebel was Deusdedit Teles de Andrade, one of those brought before the court-martial in 1912 with João Cândido, Gregório, and Dias Martins. Deusdedit was twenty years old in 1910, a white born in the state of Pernambuco, having a "rudimentary" level of schooling. Like almost all the other sailors, he was unmarried. Deusdedit was unusual in that his father's name is supplied, but his mother is unknown. Little else was recorded about him.

Reaction of the Press

What the rebel sailors had done was sensational enough to bring them to the attention of the whole Western world. Newspapers, in Brazil and elsewhere, reacted quickly to the rebellion, both reporting on it and interpreting it. The Carioca press had initially condemned the uprising that resulted in the death of naval officers. For example, the *Jornal do Brasil* ran a cartoon that shows a mourner ("the people") laying a wreath on the graves of Batista das Neves and others who were killed.[47] *O País*, the government's unofficial organ, warned that the nation's "good name" was at stake, as well as the "reputation [*fama*] of its political culture."[48] But after the amnesty, the press generally made the best of the new situation, finding merit in the rebels' behavior. The *Diário de Notícias* praised the ships' skillful evolutions. Such maneuvers would be needed in facing an enemy squadron, the paper said. In "Impressions of the City," a columnist for the *Diário* said there was widespread sympathy for "the rebels who, in view of the impossibility of freeing themselves from the slave regime . . . revolted."[49]

FonFon, a weekly magazine devoted to current events and high society, ran two cartoons in its December 3 issue, one showing a dreadnought facing a composite "foreigner," wearing a sword, pigtail, and handlebar moustaches. A second cartoon shows a battleship firing at a civilian. The cutline reads "for external use [only]." A third cartoon shows a mother scolding two boys trading blows. She says, "What will the neighbors think?" They live on Brazil Street, and around the corner stands a scowling neighbor on Argentina Street.[50] *Careta*, another Carioca magazine devoted to current events and social life, was not to be left behind. On December 10 its cover featured a cartoon about the revolt. The drawing depicted a world turned upside down, from the perspective of Brazil's racial hierarchy: Two blond sailors salute a thick-lipped and bowlegged black admiral, who wears a medal that reads "22 November 1910." Both sailors are barefoot, as was not uncommon among seamen at the time, while the "admiral" wears ill-fitting white shoes.[51]

The writer Gilberto Amado, quoted in Chapter 1 on the rush of national pride at the moment of the arrival of the *Minas* in Guanabara Bay in May 1910, later expressed his dismay at the sad attempt to achieve naval renown: "The *Minas Gerais* and the *São Paulo* were transitory emblems of a fictitious glory."[52] Was Rio de Janeiro a "mere coaling station" on the way to Buenos Aires, as the protagonist of Lima Barreto's *Rcollections of Isaías Caminha* had lamented?[53]

The sailors' revolt quickly caught the attention of leading newspapers and magazines in Europe and the United States, though the uprising had to compete with such news stories as the jailing of suffragettes in London, Francisco Madero's Mexican Revolution against Porfirio Díaz, and the funeral of Leo Tolstoy.

Foremost at issue was the nature of the rebellion. Was it "political," involving influential figures in politics and the military? The Brazilian government repeatedly denied the charge, asserting that the revolt only involved work issues of the enlisted men.[54] *Le Temps* in Paris, the *New York Times*, and James Bryce, the British ambassador to the United States, who was in Rio at the moment of the revolt, agreed.[55] The *New York Times* and *Outlook*, an influential weekly to which Theodore Roosevelt frequently contributed, both called it a "labor strike."[56] But the Brazilian government went further: it conveniently omitted corporal punishment from its list of sailors' grievances in statements to the foreign press.[57] Nonetheless, foreign papers quickly picked up the main issue, and a *New York Times* headline on November 28, 1910, stated, "Sailors had been tortured." The paper even interviewed a Brazilian sailor named A. Daromes, who said he had participated in the plot on the *Minas Gerais*, but he had deserted before the uprising. He spoke of frequent floggings and continuous labor lasting up to thirty-six hours.[58]

Acknowledging the charge of brutality, an anonymous "patriote bresilien" in Paris played to French prejudices. He wrote in *Le Matin* that the naval revolt had resulted from the cruelties of "Prussian militarism" that the German-influenced Brazilian army had passed on to the navy. The same argument appeared in *Gil Blas*.[59] The dilemma of what the government should do, once the sailors had control of the dreadnoughts, elicited different opinions abroad. *Le Temps* argued that the government should have starved the crews out—waiting until their supplies of coal, water, and food were exhausted, but David Lambuth, an American eyewitness to the rebellion, said that the policy had been tried and had failed. Writing in the New York-based magazine *The Independent*, Lambuth stated that the government had sent a water barge to the *Minas Gerais* when

João Cândido threatened to destroy the Ilha das Cobras, and during the revolt the *Deodoro* had taken on coal at Niteroi, while local guards fled.[60]

When the government surrendered to the rebels' demands, *The Spectator*, an influential weekly in London, acknowledged that Hermes had had little choice, facing the potential devastation of Rio.[61] Most foreign media agreed. *Le Temps* speculated that Hermes's government feared that not ending the revolt quickly might tempt discontented elements in the military to join in. Lambuth in *The Independent* and an anonymous writer in *Outlook* believed that saving the costly dreadnoughts had been a decisive motive, and, indeed, these aims were at the core of Rio Branco's South American diplomatic strategy.[62] But foreign observers unanimously held that the Brazilian government had suffered an enormous blow to its prestige. *Le Temps* said that only the opposition could profit from the instability the amnesty "solution" had provided; *Outlook* spoke of the complete "humiliation and mortification" of the government; *The Spectator* lamented that "the submission of such mutineers [was] . . . got only by purchasing it"; and another London weekly, *The Nation*, said Brazil's two dreadnoughts were now "something worse than white elephants."[63]

In his diatribe *Política vs. Marinha*, the anonymous "Officer of the Navy" (José Eduardo de Macedo Soares) probably exaggerated when he claimed that in the musical revues at the Moulin Rouge and the Folies Bergère, the outcome of the Brazilian revolt was the "object of laughter and merriment."[64] In any case, censure verging on ridicule by the foreign press was real. The American magazine *Current Literature* commented that it was "ignominious" for the officers on the rebel-dominated ships to let themselves "be put ashore like schoolboys."[65] The *New York Times* called the government's surrender "disgraceful," but, looking inward, asked in an editorial: What if US sailors should threaten to destroy New York? Surely local officials would plead with Washington not to sacrifice their city "to the dignity of the government."[66]

Foreign admiration for the organization of the revolt and the piloting skills of the rebels, plus a general sympathy for the abolition of whipping, was widespread, and seemingly unanimous. The US chargé d'affaires thought the rebels showed themselves "competent to maneuver [the dreadnoughts] with exceptional skill."[67] *Le Figaro* admired the sailors' "precision of maneuvering the enormous warships" in spite of the absence of officers.[68] *Current Literature*, based on the account of a reporter for the London *Daily Telegraph*, even said the battleships were "better handled," after the officers were forced to leave.[69] And the US military attaché for South America said the Brazilian ships "were handled in a manner that was nothing short of wonderful, considering that the commanders in every case were seamen." In fact, he believed the "sailors had been well instructed," and João Cândido had "proved that there is excellent ability in the Brazilian ranks."[70]

In an age of strong race prejudice, *Collier's*, another popular American magazine, paid this tribute: "Without officers . . . fifteen hundred blacks had for four days successfully handled and maneuvered the largest modern warships afloat, made use of their wireless apparatus, and manipulated their big guns. They had defied the Government of Brazil, and . . . had been able to dictate to the President."[71]

Some of the newspaper reports overstated the sailors' nautical skills, understandably, since they were only able to observe the handling of the ships in the bay. The rebel seamen could not "navigate," as was reported in some newspapers, because operating the ships on the high seas involved skills the sailors did not possess. They could only "govern" the ships, moving them in familiar waters, in and out of the bay, as good helmsmen. Likewise, although they were able to fire the largest cannons on the dreadnoughts, they didn't have the skill to aim them accurately, but probably just fired point-blank into the city.[72] That was enough, however, to achieve their purposes.

Argentine leaders had a special interest in the events of the naval rebellion since Argentina had followed Brazil's lead in purchasing dreadnoughts—in their case, in the United States. *La Prensa*, the country's leading newspaper, had its own correspondent in Rio. The paper noted that Britain's Admiral Farquahar had weighed anchor in the Rio de la Plata to proceed to Rio de Janeiro, and it gave extensive coverage to the events there. *La Prensa* reported the account of Brazilian journalist Júlio Medeiros that João Cândido was given the honors of an admiral by his fellow seamen. It furthermore summarized reactions to the uprising in London, Paris, New York, and Berlin.[73] One may suppose a general *schadenfreude* prevailed among Argentine statesmen and naval officers regarding the revolt, but possibly with this disturbing afterthought: If ordinary sailors could operate the main ships of the squadron so well without their officers, couldn't they also do that in battle with their potential antagonist? In fact, the US military attaché in Buenos Aires, who also had responsibility for Brazil, noted that the Brazilian sailors' skillful maneuvers gave the lie to the Argentine officers' presumption that the seamen couldn't handle a dreadnought.[74] And if Argentine naval officers had been aware of the fraternization between their own sailors and their Brazilian counterparts (as reported by "Ex-sailor"), they might also have been concerned about a mutiny in the Argentine fleet. "Ex-sailor" furthermore claims that Dias Martins gained the support of Argentine sailors for the intended revolt during the period September 9 to 20, when the *Bahia* was anchored in the port of Buenos Aires.[75]

The Significance of Corporal Punishment

Two weeks after the revolt, a letter appeared in the *Jornal do Comércio*, shedding light on the causes of the uprising. Dated December 2, 1910, it was a statement by the interim commander of the cruiser *Bahia* during its voyage to Chile. The ship had been sent there to participate in that country's celebration of a hundred years of independence. During the trip, Captain Alberto Durão Coelho had ordered a sailor to undergo fifteen lashes for disrespecting the quartermaster of the ship. Following the incident, on September 1, Coelho received an anonymous letter to the effect that sailors, too, ought to enjoy the respect of their officers. Twenty years after the founding of the republic, the letter pointed out, they were still subject to the lash. Coelho was told he should remember the battleship *Potemkin*, whose crew had successfully revolted against the imperial Russian government five years earlier. "Take care, if you want to see your family again," the note warned. There was a "'black hand'" or "union of honor" on the ship. "It is not only the higher-ups [*os grandes*] who create the greatness of the pátria; we also . . . contribute to its greatness. . . . We have nothing to lose." The commander discovered that the handwriting matched that of the keeper of the armory (*paioleiro*), Francisco Dias Martins, who had never been flogged. In Coelho's opinion, Dias Martins was worthy of the responsible post he held. On the trip Coelho administered corporal punishment to seven men, but he didn't say whether any floggings had occurred after the note was delivered to him. In any event, the ship was seriously understaffed, wrote Coelho, resulting in an extremely laborious journey for the seamen; 70 percent of them were illiterate, he said, implying that this fact lowered their efficiency.[76]

For the Brazilian government, the sailors' revolt was ostensibly, at least primarily, a "job action," or more euphemistically, a grievance about work rules. But for the participants in the movement, it was far more than that. Whipping was not just a form of maintaining discipline, but a barbaric form of punishment that had strong and negative historical associations. Slavery had grown increasingly moribund in the 1880s, and parliament banned whipping in public places in 1886. As observed earlier, Brazil only abolished slavery in 1888, making it the last country in the Western Hemisphere to do so. Moreover, flogging was a formal event that officers and men were all obliged to witness. The command structure justified it as a form of legitimate punishment that could be used to mete out justice aboard ship, thus avoiding long delays that a military hearing ashore would involve. Once the flogging had been administered and the sailor had recovered, he could be employed again on ships that were chronically short-handed.

Naval officers, such as Heitor Pereira da Cunha, who was present during the Revolt of the Whip and later rose to commander, wrote that it was impossible to maintain discipline without corporal punishment.[77] The anonymous "Officer of the Navy" agreed, given what he alleged was the base morality of the crewmen.[78] Other officers justified corporal punishment by asserting that sailors wanted to prove their indifference to pain before both their superiors and their fellow sailors. In the words of a Brazilian admiral in 1961:

> our seamen of that time, lacking the moral and intellectual requirements for appreciating the debasing aspect of the punishment [whipping], accepted it naturally, as an opportunity to show their physical and moral superiority. . . . All this is . . . understandable in the face of the backward mentality and ignorance of the personnel that composed the ships' crews.[79]

But the sailors' demands in 1910 show that the admiral was wrong. That whipping and related forms of corporal punishment—such as the use of the *palmatória*, a paddle used to beat the palms of the hands of sailors, and formerly those of slaves—were the main grievance is shown by the frequency and ranking of this demand compared to the others.[80] Flogging was a form of torture—as the headline in the *New York Times* had indicated—and was designed to humiliate the victim. Its application showed the man punished was a person without honor. Officers were not whipped. In addition, Brazilian sailors were well aware that sailors in other navies were no longer flogged. The last European power to abolish corporal punishment was Russia in 1904. And "Ex-sailor" makes a point that the humiliation of flogging could be international: on the *Bahia's* voyage to Chile in September 1910, not only were crewmen whipped, but in one case a sailor's pants were stripped off and he was paddled on the hips—in the sight of Chilean and US ships' crews at Valparaíso, the port of Santiago.[81] João Cândido, in his "memories" of 1912, also refers to this event and claims that fourteen Brazilian sailors were subjected to whipping during the trip.[82] Flogging was the grievance that produced briefer mutinies in the Brazilian navy off the port of Rio Grande in 1893 and another off Gibraltar in 1904.[83]

But humiliation and outrage at injustice do not alone produce rebellion. There was a possible model for a naval revolt. It was supplied by the men as well as the officers of the Portuguese navy when the *São Paulo* had been in Lisbon, six weeks before the November 22 rising. The *Adamastor*, the ship on which the Portuguese Republican revolution began more or less simultaneously with a revolt in the city of Lisbon, had come to Rio for Hermes's inauguration, and on that occasion, fraternization probably occurred between Portuguese and Brazilian sailors. Anecdotal evidence to this effect, is found in the Carioca weekly, *Careta*:

> The sailor of the *Adamastor*: How did it happen, mate, here in Guanabara Bay?
>
> The sailor of the *São Paulo*: We all remembered what we saw on the Tagus—the *Adamastor* with its banner of the victorious revolution—and so we did the same thing.
>
> —Then, we, over there, were rooting for you.
>
> —And we, over here, were rooting for you. We turned everything upside down.[84]

Fraternization might also be surmised from the fact that the Brazilian rebels informed the ship *Adamastor* of their intent to bomb Brazilian targets.

A few contemporary observers also speculated that there was a connection between the two revolts.[85] Another "bad example" was the behavior of the British stokers on the *Minas Gerais'* maiden voyage. They went on strike against Captain Batista das Neves and were landed at Hampton Roads, Virginia, sacrificing their pay.[86]

Other cleavages in the navy complicated the story. One was that between the *florianistas* (supporters of President Floriano Peixoto) and the "monarchist" rebels in 1893–94, many of whom were not monarchists, but simply officers opposed to a general-turned-president whom they considered a dictator. Among them was Admiral Eduardo Wandenkolk, the republic's first minister of the navy. Although the officers who rebelled were mostly reabsorbed into the navy after the movement failed in 1895, the divisions were not forgotten. The minister who proposed the naval rearmament program in 1904, Júlio César de Noronha, had been loyal to President Floriano Peixoto in the 1890s, as had been Joaquim Marques de Leão, the minister at the time of the 1910 revolt. But Alexandrino de Alencar, the minister between their tenures who would again be minister from 1913 to 1918, had been a rebel in 1893. He nullified some of Leão's reforms resulting from the events of 1910 when he returned to office.

Another division was a generational one, combined with the demands of new technology as the Brazilian navy passed from windpower to steampower and then to the dreadnoughts. Older officers and sailors did not adapt easily to the modern steel vessels.[87] As H. L. Martins points out, although João Cândido belonged to the older group trained on sailing vessels, he had taken instruction in England to handle dreadnoughts. His skill as helmsman on the new battleships duly impressed the younger crewmen who had been trained on steel ships. It was the younger generation—men in their early twenties—who supplied most of the leadership of the revolt against the whip. Like their seniors, they found flogging insupportable, in part because of its association with the slave regime. The two groups shared the grievance of overwork because dreadnought-class vessels required around-the-clock maintenance and did not afford lengthy moments of leisure known to sailors on the wind-powered ships or older ironclad steamships. The younger men, especially those who had been given specialized training in England, probably considered their seniors valiant but ignorant.[88]

Officers lagged behind their counterparts in other modern navies in their condescending views of noncoms (*suboficiais*) and machinists, whom they saw as servants or practitioners of "demeaning" forms of manual labor.[89] As observed, the machinists were formally officers, but were considered to be contracted technicians: they were not combat officers and could not aspire to leadership posts in the navy. In the November rebellion, therefore, they tended to assume a neutral position in the struggle between officers and men.[90] Meanwhile in Britain, First Sea Lord John ("Jackie") Fisher had begun to improve the conditions of men of "the lower deck" in 1906—the year the original dreadnought was produced—by providing ordinary seamen better pay and victualing the following

year. In the process, he improved their morale and gave them a sense of
pride of membership in a corporate body, His Majesty's Royal Navy.[91]
Brazilian sailors training in Britain at Newcastle-on-Tyne (Armstrong-
Whitworth) or at Barrow-in-Furness (Vickers), where the *São Paulo* had
been built, felt that they too deserved respect, as indicated in their decla-
rations in the November crisis.

Were the sailors, or their leaders, motivated by any formal ideology?
"Ideology" is a hard term to define, but the formal radical ideologies that
may have been available to Brazilian sailors were anarchism (particularly
that of Mikhail Bakunin and Errico Malatesta, the latter having lived in
South America) and Marxism. Anarchism influenced labor groups in Rio
de Janeiro, where Portuguese, Spanish, and Italian immigrants were active in Brazilian workers' associations. Naval Minister Leão, in his annual
report to the president for 1910, stated that the revolted Brazilian seamen
had picked up "the subversive ideas of a poorly understood libertarian-
ism" through their contacts with foreign sailors during their training in
Europe.[92] But anarchist rhetoric and discourse are absent from the dec-
larations in the sailors' "memorial" and in the telegrams sent from the
rebels' ships.

Marxism seems even more remote as a source of ideological inspira-
tion. Again, in the rebels' manifestoes there is no reference to terms like
"working class" or "bourgeoisie," and Marxism had almost no expression in Brazil until after the formation of the Communist International
in 1919.[93] Sailors elsewhere, however, had been influenced by Marxism,
most famously in the 1905 rebellion of the Russian battleship *Potemkin* off
the city of Odessa. Constantine Feldmann, a (Marxist) Social Democrat
helped push the crew to revolutionary action. The rebels took the *Potemkin* to Constanza, Romania, where they obtained asylum.

Ideology follows trade routes, and Brazilian seamen had traveled widely
and learned about the revolt of the *Potemkin*, however well or poorly they
understood its causes and ideological foundations.[94] Gregório, the "commander" of the *São Paulo*, had indeed been around the world. Contact
with radicalized Russian sailors is made more plausible by the fact that
thirty-seven of the *Potemkin*'s crew apparently ended up in Buenos Aires
in September 1908.[95] Francisco Dias Martins, who had been in Buenos
Aires in September 1910, en route from Chile to Rio de Janeiro, had
referred to the Potemkin incident in his anonymous note to Captain
Coelho: "Remember the Russian squadron in the Baltic."[96] He had con-

fused the Baltic with the Black Sea and had said nothing about particular demands or aspirations of the Russian rebels, thus referring to the Russian case only as an example of a successful mutiny against injustice.

João Cândido and Dias Martins—if we may identify the "Ex-sailor" with the latter—were the only two participants in the revolt who left any extended testimony about the rebellion, and their references to formal ideology are nonexistent.[97] True, in his interview with the journalist Hélio Silva in 1968, the year before his death, João Cândido referred to the sailors' conspiratorial groups as "revolutionary committees," implying something more than a job action, though it is likely that this phrase derives from Cândido's acquaintance with politicized sailors long after the 1910 rebellion. According to Cândido's testimony in 1968, the rebels didn't want to register a protest, but to "impose" a solution.[98] Of course, the enormity of the grievance of flogging and the loss of life during the struggle may have justified the term "revolutionary" in Cândido's mind, but it seems likely that "revolutionary committees" was a term that he had picked up from radical seamen in the early 1960s.

In 1911 the Liga Marítima Brasileira, an officers' association, denied the rebellion was inspired by any ideology whatsoever in "Discipline aboard [the ship]," following the mutiny. For the Liga, the Brazilian crews were extremely "malleable" and "impulsive," living in a state of "super-excitement" that gave rise to rebellion. Their chief concern was food, said the Liga. But rotten meat was the spark that had set off the *Potemkin* revolt. Referring to the *Potemkin*, the Liga Marítima asserted that the Russian sailors in 1905 who bombed Odessa and the commanders of the rebellious Portuguese cruisers who bombed Lisbon in October 1910 had political (implicitly, ideological) motives. The Brazilian sailors did not have that excuse.[99] The publication made no mention of flogging as a cause of the rebellion. President Hermes in his annual report to Congress in 1912 also omitted reference to whipping as a grievance. He declared that the naval revolt's "principal if not sole cause" was "the lack of moral culture of the majority of our sailors."[100]

But the rebellion, far from being just a job grievance, did have strong ideological foundations, even though they were less novel than anarchism and Marxism. The degree to which the ideology of the revolted sailors tapped into, or were influenced by, Brazilian traditions of popular radicalism is not easy to determine. The memory of Jacobin tradition of the 1890s probably lived on among the officers who rejected the corrupt oligarchies of their home states—basically, extended families—and called themselves "Salvationists" in the Hermes years,[101] but there is no evidence that Jacobinism as ideology or mentality affected the sailors of 1910. Their reformism concerned their own claims to rights as citizens and to the brutal working conditions they faced; they did not attempt to change broader political institutions or practices. Their perception of their own situation was influenced by what they understood about working conditions of other seafarers—most notably the British, with whom they necessarily associated to learn their new jobs. But the labor practices they saw at Newcastle and Barrow were inextricably associated with British seamen's rights and the respect British officers accorded to the lower deck.

As for resorting to direct action and willingness to contemplate violence, the rebel sailors may have been affected by Brazilian officers' actions in the 1890s or by various military uprisings later. Many of the sailors on the *São Paulo* had witnessed the naval revolt against the Portuguese monarchy. But, given the average age of both leaders and followers, any memory of the illegal activities of abolitionists in the 1880s seem even more doubtful than the more recent Jacobin movement. During the Revolt of the Whip, one radiogram referred to the sailors who were "enslaved" by the officers. Immediately following this assertion came the statement that the plight of the seamen wasn't a matter of "politics, but of the rights of the miserable sailors."[102]

The ideology or "mentality" or "outlook" of the sailors, inchoate as it may have been, ultimately derived from the statement of the Rights of Man by the French revolutionaries of 1789. Brazilian sailors considered themselves citizens under the Republican constitution of 1891. Under that constitution, habeas corpus was used to get boys out of the naval apprentice schools, and this helped strengthen a consciousness among sailors of the rights of citizenship. In 1903 a decree regulating the draft lottery affecting sailors in the merchant marine was challenged by a riot in Fortaleza, the capital of Ceará, while a strike of maritime workers broke out in Rio. Several sailors asked for a writ of habeas corpus and received it, even though the Supreme Court declared the lottery legal.[103]

Despite sailors' demands for the recognition of their rights as citizens, it must be noted that, unlike their officers, the seamen were denied the right to vote—most of them doubly so. They were specifically denied suffrage because of their position in the armed forces, just like enlisted men in the army. And the fact that the majority were illiterate was a second reason why they were not considered full citizens, with the right of suffrage, under the constitution. Among those who had spent the most time acquiring new skills in England, such as the (necessarily literate) radio telegraphers, discontent was probably greatest. They were well aware of the recent improvements in the living and working conditions of common seamen in Britain.[104]

The Belle Époque was a period in which the right to universal male suffrage was sweeping across Europe, and the sailors probably didn't realize that suffrage was the key to eventual political power for the masses, and therefore one of the most important rights of citizenship.[105] In the view of one historian, the fact that the citizens' rights issue, which appeared prominently in the manifesto of November 23, later was obscured in the effort to end corporal punishment, should be seen as a deliberate political act. The sailors considered themselves "citizens in uniform" with the right to demand the dismissal of incompetent officers, the reformulation of the code of discipline, an increase in wages, training and education, and the reduction of work schedules. The movement, among other things, was an effort to establish modern labor relations in the navy and to professionalize the ranks. The sailors believed that as citizens, they could make claims on the state in line with their legitimate rights.[106]

The desire for "freedom," a slogan of the revolt and a manifest right of all citizens, probably has its origins in the memory of slavery, as it apparently was for Carioca stevedores in their strike of 1906.[107] Another strike of naval mechanics broke out in Recife in 1909. At the same time, specialist groups—such as stokers and coal suppliers (*carvoeiros*) were forming their own national associations, a fact that testified to the growing professionalization among sailors.[108] This trend, especially among those who had received dreadnought training in England, may have resulted in frustration when noncitizens (for example, Portuguese stowaways on the *Bahia*'s Atlantic voyage), were recruited to supply the chronically insufficient manpower needs of the new capital ships.[109]

But the defense of citizen-sailors' rights "across the board" may have been a maximum aspiration, around which bargaining might take place. There was nothing like a uniform and inalterable position among the sailors. In the November 22 uprising, uncoordinated demands came from different ships, and on November 24, two days after the mutiny began, the "rebels" sent a radiogram saying, "We do not want to harm anyone. We only want a pay raise, without flogging."[110] We know there may have been dissension about the peace terms after they were voted by Congress, and the unified front for broad citizens' rights collapsed, or had never been agreed on. The extent to which a coherent ideology and program was achieved can probably be credited to the radio operators, notably Ricardo Freitas. The insubordination of one of those radio telegraphers, Scipião Zanotti, would cost him his life.

§4 The Second Revolt and its Consequences

On the day following the navy's resumption of control of the rebel ships, November 27, officers supervised the removal of the breeches from the largest guns. After the amnesty, tensions understandably remained high between officers and enlisted men, a fact noted by João Cândido himself in his "Memories," published in 1913. Some of the sailors even feared being executed.[1] Underlying the relationship was the desire for revenge of the officers on those who had killed their peers on the night of November 22. On some of the ships that had remained loyal to the government, crews had wavered in the crisis, and commanders no longer trusted their men who, having benefited from the success of the first revolt, might themselves take part in a second insurrection. Evidence was not long in coming. A letter from a sailor named Nazário Damião addressed to Dias Martins, dated November 29, concerned an uprising against officers in Amazonas. Thus, only a week after the mutiny, sailors were considering action against their superiors half a continent away from the capital.[2]

Meanwhile, discipline had broken down on the ships whose crews had revolted, as exemplified by the fact that on the *Minas Gerais*, João Cândido remained an informal commander: the sailors on the ship only obeyed orders that he had approved.[3] When called to muster, few men appeared for the lineup. Furthermore, two officers were denied permission by sailors to enter the *Minas* in the days following the amnesty.[4] On their side, many seamen were dissatisfied that no immediate pay raise came with the agreement to turn over the ships to the government—although a bill authored by Senator Pires Ferreira to that effect was approved by Congress early in 1911.[5] Additionally, nothing specific had been promised about improving working conditions and rations. Worst of all, perhaps, was the fact that, although floggings were no longer applied, no decree or statute resulted from the revolt that formally forbade the practice. A bill to prohibit whipping was drafted by two opposition senators from São Paulo, Francisco Glicério and Alfredo Ellis, but it was not enacted into law.[6] Naval Minister Leão procured the services of the renowned jurist Clóvis Bevelaqua to edit a new penal code for the navy, but a new set of laws would only be implemented in 1923. And it did not explicitly abolish corporal punishment. In the words of the naval historian H. L. Martins, "flogging simply disappeared, its abolition verified in the codes and regulations elaborated later."[7]

In fact, there was an unacknowledged but little-known model for this procedure from the most powerful navy in the world. The use of the infamous cat-o-nine-tails in the British navy, though terminated in 1881, was still technically permitted—in theory up to forty-eight strokes—in the regulations of 1939! An authority on the British lower deck at the turn of the century writes:

> In practice flogging had been *suspended* as a punishment in 1881 (not abolished, as in the army), but if it was no longer used, the Admiralty clung to it as a deterrent.[8] All ships carried a cat as a reminder of what might be: the Admiralty retained the right to sanction its use without parliamentary approval, and flogging continued as a recognized punishment in naval prisons.[9] Moreover, for boys, the British Navy permitted caning and birching (in which blood was drawn) as late as the 1920s.[10]

Another interpretation of the termination of Brazil's corporal punishment, expressed by a retired admiral, was that it was one side of an implicit bargain: in 1910 the navy's right to flog its enlistees was exchanged for the right to exclude sailors from the navy without a formal dismissal process, which had been in effect up to that time.[11]

Whatever the reasoning—or rationalization—of the Brazilian admiralty regarding the cessation of flogging, many of the sailors in 1910 were not satisfied with the amnesty. These included a group of radicals on the *Minas*—among them João José do Nascimento, the killer of Commander Batista das Neves, and the sailor who urinated on his corpse, Aristides Pereira (Chaminé, or "Chimney"). This group now styled themselves the *faixas pretas* (black bands) because they wore their black kerchiefs like Sam Browne belts. They accused João Cândido of siding with the officers against the men. And in fact, according to João Cândido's later testimony, he did supply a list of unreliable personnel to naval authorities.[12]

Using this and many other sources of information, the government pressed the advantage it had gained in repossessing its most powerful ships: On November 28, only two days after the revolt had ended, Naval Minister Leão violated the agreement not to take reprisals against the rebels and their sympathizers: he signed Decree 8400, which illegally bypassed the Disciplinary Council (Conselho de Disciplina) and permitted the systematic and peremptory "exclusion" of sailors from the navy. On December 2, the police arrested eight sailors for conspiracy on the Rua do Lavradio, in the downtown area. On the 4th, another twenty-two were arrested in Piedade, farther west in the Zona Norte, where most of the working class lived. Ninety-eight more men in the Naval Battalion were taken prisoner on the 6th.[13] Two days later, the navy began the process of dismissing seamen on a name-by-name basis, including the killer of Batista das Neves. The same day, Dias Martins—who, perhaps anticipating a crackdown, had already asked for a discharge—was among those to be removed from the *Bahia*. A letter revealing a plot to mutiny, also dated December 8, fell into the hands of the authorities.[14]

Did these measures, in whole or in part, constitute a deliberate provocation by the government? No surviving records establish such an hypothesis. The government may or may not have set such a trap. Yet, given the mutual antagonism between officers and men, the success of the first rebellion, and the breakdown of discipline on the capital ships, the authorities had every reason to foresee, and plan for, a second uprising. There is little need to search for a "smoking gun" that would establish a provocation; such an event was in the logic of the situation. It seems likely that President Hermes heeded Rio Branco's implicit suggestion that the government could emulate Pitt the Younger, who had crushed the second rebellion in the British navy in 1797.

Even if the authorities intended to provoke a second mutiny through the sausage-slicing tactics of case-by-case dismissals, its immediate purpose was obviously to purge the navy of potential rebels, starting with those who were most suspect. In any event, such events did not produce a reaction among the crews that had rebelled in November. Rather, it was the sailors of the cruiser *Rio Grande do Sul*, the sister ship of the *Bahia*, who rebelled on the evening of December 9, the day after the crews of the *Minas* and the *Bahia* had been purged. The captain of the *Rio Grande*,

Pedro Max de Frontin, however, had been forewarned of the revolt and
passed the information up the chain of command. But the chief of the
navy's general staff ignored the report,[15] giving rise to the suspicion that
the government wanted a second rebellion to occur. During the rising,
which broke out about 8:30 p.m., Frontin reestablished his authority after
a thirty-minute struggle in which both a sailor and a Lieutenant-Captain,
Francisco Xavier Carneiro da Cunha, died.[16]

Another and more dangerous rebellion broke out in a land-based unit
almost simultaneously, pointing to coordination of the two events. The
Naval Battalion (marines, or naval fusiliers) rose up against their superiors
in the barracks of the fort on the Ilha das Cobras.[17] The battalion was
a unit of the Brazilian army assigned to the navy. Like the sailors, the
enlisted men in the Naval Battalion were overwhelmingly of African or
partly African ancestry. According to the historian Capanema, in 1908,
the battalion was composed of 32 percent blacks, 45 percent *pardos* (mixed
race), and 20 percent whites. Or more simply, 79 percent were nonwhite,
the same share she found for the navy, though the share of "blacks" (*pretos*) was almost three times as great.[18]

On the evening of December 9, members of the 3rd and 5th companies
of the Naval Battalion cut the lights and telephone lines. They seized
control of the armory, distributed weapons, freed prisoners, and occupied the central enclosure of the fort, bringing artillery and machine guns
with them. In all, they seized six 12-pounder landing guns, four Hotchkiss
automatic machine guns, and two hundred fifty Mauser rifles.[19] Officers
were roped off in one corner. The commander of the Naval Battalion,
Francisco Marques da Rocha, was taken by surprise because of his faith in
the loyalty of the troops, despite having been warned of a revolt by a police official.[20] His subordinate, Sergeant Antero José Marques,[21] organized
a bayonet charge against the revolted troops, but was forced to withdraw.
A majority of the battalion's soldiers—about two hundred—did not revolt, however, and took refuge in the naval hospital on the island.[22]

The government set up field pieces along the waterfront opposite the
Ilha das Cobras, including the Cais Pharoux, and at the naval arsenal on
the Ilha das Cobras. At 5 a.m., military forces on the mainland opened an
attack on the island fort, and the rebels fired back. Panic broke out in the
city on the night of December 9–10, just as it had on November 23.[23] The
mutinous marines used their cannons to attack the Naval Arsenal and the
army battery on the Morro de São Bento, overlooking the island. Their

12-pounder cannons were designed as naval guns for use ashore and had short barrels. They were less powerful than the shore battery the government possessed. The navy brought up the loyal battleship *Floriano*, the sister ship of the *Deodoro*, the cruisers *Barroso* and *Tamoio*, and the newly minted *Rio Grande do Sul*, after its commander had quelled the mutiny aboard.[24] According to the American military attaché, they all fired wildly off the mark,[25] but a government howitzer on the Morro finally scored a direct hit on the rebels' artillery. Further barrages by the battery and other loyal forces reduced the fort to rubble. During the hostilities, General Antônio Mena Barreto, soon to be minister of war, was wounded. Many rebels fled the carnage by attempting to escape in small boats during the night, but loyal destroyers, on the lookout for them, took many prisoners.[26] The government continued to bomb the fort several hours after the mutineers raised a white flag. The prolonged attack may have had the goal of forcing Congress to approve a state of siege.[27] When the army took possession of the fort, seventeen hours after the revolt began, rebel casualties included twenty-three dead and eighteen wounded.[28] As a result of the bombing, the fort and barracks lay in ruins, and the commander's house had been destroyed.

More violence followed: a massacre after the surrender—unmentioned in the Brazilian sources—was reported by a British naval officer and passed on to the US chargé d'affaires in Buenos Aires: "Yesterday evening the mutineers came out of their holes [on the Ilha das Cobras] where they had been hiding from the gunfire, and capitulated. A certain number were shot at once, two were seen from our ships to be taken on board one of the Brazilian men-of-war [the *Floriano*?] and then and there shot on deck."[29] There were also casualties ashore, including civilians.

The navy's Court of Inquiry (Conselho de Investigação), a kind of grand jury, held a hearing on the Naval Battalion uprising. It determined that the leaders of the rebellion had been Sergeant Benedito Rodrigues de Oliveira, aided by Corporal Jesuíno Leme de Carvalho, known in the barracks as "Piaba." They had the support of some forty-five other sergeants and corporals.[30] Unlike the court-martial's records on the navy's role in the second uprising, the records of the Court of Inquiry's investigation of the Naval Battalion revolt seem to have disappeared, a fact that raises speculation about whether there was a cover-up.[31]

The fact that no officers were implicated in the second revolt did not preclude the possibility that civilians had been involved. Inevitably, the issue arose of whether there was a "political" motive in the uprising that would implicate powerful politicians. A civil police investigation in April 1912 concerning both the November and the December revolts, included interviews with former rebels, among them Francisco Dias Martins and João Cândido. Both, and the investigators as well, answered the question in the negative.[32]

No formal statement survives of what the insurgent marines wanted; in the barracks on the Ilha das Cobras they had shouted cries of "freedom" and demands for an end to unspecified grievances resulting from "rote practices" (*carrancismo*), perhaps referring to gymnastic exercises. Another cause might be the arrest of ninety-eight of their fellow marines on December 6. One historian thinks that the second uprising was a response to unendurable working and living conditions,[33] but a report by the US military attaché, based on an inspection of the barracks just days before the rebellion, contradicts that judgment. Lt. John S. Hammond, the US military attaché for South America, was the guest of the commander of the Naval Battalion, Marques da Rocha, on December 5. He found the men neat and "smart in appearance. . . . The barracks were spotlessly clean." The soldiers had good rations, new rifles, and modern equipment. Marques da Rocha's claim to Hammond that the "men were contented, the discipline excellent, and the battalion faithful . . . to its officers" was, for the American officer, "very believable."[34] Until further evidence is discovered, the grievances that motivated the rebels will remain unknown, though the first rebellion showed that mutinies could succeed.

And what of the former rebels, when the second rebellion broke out at sea on the *Rio Grande*, and at the fort? In the words of naval historian Martins, "Everything indicates that the leaders in the previous movement, on the *Minas Gerais*, the *São Paulo*, the *Bahia*, and the *Deodoro* . . . were caught by surprise."[35] The crews of the two floating fortresses as well as the other former rebel-held ships in fact remained loyal to the government and their officers aboard the ships. The *São Paulo* and the *Minas Gerais* might have made short work of the rebels had they been able to use their largest guns. However, because the breeches had been removed after the November revolt, the former rebels, now loyal again to their commanders, could only use smaller weapons.

The loyalty of crews who had overpowered their officers on November 22 was tested, however, when emissaries of the mutineers of the *Rio Grande do Sul* reported an atrocity. Approaching both dreadnoughts in

launches, they falsely alleged that inÏantry units had massacred the revolted sailors on the *Rio Grande*. This "information" produced something
approaching panic among sailors on the two largest ships. Fear spread
from men to the officers: the former dreaded the overwhelming force
of military units, while the latter feared preemptive violence by seamen
against themselves. At this point, the interim commander (*imediato*) on
the *Minas Gerais*, Lieutenant-Commander Henrique Saddock da Sá, noting the indecision of the crew, contacted the captain of the *Minas Gerais*,
Pereira Leite, who apparently was ashore. With the latter's approval,
Saddock ordered the officers off the ship, leaving João Cândido in charge
of the *Minas Gerais*. Cândido pleaded with Saddock to stay, but in vain.[36]
Cândido and Gregório, once more in charge of the *São Paulo* after the officers had retired from that ship, reported this fact to the minister of the
navy, saying they awaited further orders. The two battleships exchanged
messages, agreeing that they should not revolt.[37]

Cândido radioed the Naval Ministry that the officers had left the
Minas, and that he was in charge, as on November 22. The message was
signed by "the crew." Gregório again led the *São Paulo* under similar circumstances, though the second dreadnought's telegram professing loyalty to the government was signed by Commander Silvinato Moura, still
aboard the ship.[38] One of the problems for both the navy and the loyal
leadership of the amnestied sailors was the conflicting radiograms passed
among the warships, only some of which were known to João Cândido.
Messages of which he was unaware may have included some sent from the
Minas itself.[39]

By radiogram Cândido asked for, but did not receive, the replacement
of the gun magazines to suppress the rebellion.[40] The navy did not want
to risk those same shells being used against the government. Cândido
received a message directly from Catete, the presidential palace, demanding that the two great ships remain loyal to the government. As proof of
his loyalty, Cândido reported that he had refused entry on the *Minas* by a
messenger from the Naval Battalion.[41] Told to support the government's
action against the new uprising, the former rebels did so, firing a 120mm
cannon, the shells for which had been successfully hidden from the government crews who had removed the large gun breeches.

Meanwhile the howitzers on São Bento continued to rain shells on
the barracks on Ilha das Cobras, and shrapnel from one such projectile
wounded João Cândido in the heel. The radicals on the *Minas Gerais*, led

by Aristides Pereira (Chaminé) and Vitalino José Ferreira (a killer of an officer on that ship in the first revolt), seeing the danger to the ship and its crew, brandished revolvers and demanded that Cândido move the warship out of range of the shore batteries. He did so willingly, for the same reason, heading for the Ilha do Viana to take on coal, about 3 p.m. on December 10.[42] In the meantime, the minister of the navy ordered Pereira Leite, Saddock, and other officers of the *Minas* back on the ship.[43] But Cândido had already moved the dreadnought to the small island.

When the officers of the *Minas Gerais* finally reboarded, Cândido explained why he had moved the ship, giving them copies of radiograms of which he had knowledge. Commander Pereira Leite ordered the crew to attention and praised them for their loyalty. However, when the captain of the *São Paulo* withdrew from that ship with his officers, Pereira Leite asked for permission to do likewise on the *Minas Gerais*. The naval minister assented and appointed José Borges Leite commander of the ship.[44] He assumed command at 5 p.m., and João Cândido retired to the sick bay to dress his wounded heel. Meanwhile, Pereira Leite was named director of the Battleship Division by the minister of the navy, in what was perhaps a face-saving promotion.[45] Elsewhere, Borges Leite on December 11 was already asking to be relieved of command of the *Minas*, probably because of the lack of qualified personnel and low morale among crew and officers.[46] On the several formerly rebel-held ships, the sailors who had objected to João Cândido's "soft" leadership continued to challenge his unofficial but implicit authority. The situation changed on December 12, three days after the second rebellion had begun. The navy now told all officers to leave their ships; the enlisted men were to follow them. Cândido came out of sick bay to persuade the sailors to obey, but he failed.

The majority of the sailors on the *Minas Gerais*, João Cândido later stated, wanted confirmation that the president had really ordered them to quit the ship.[47] Perhaps they viewed the order as a violation of the amnesty. But Naval Minister Leão radioed back that the government demanded obedience and would attack the *Minas*, and even sink it, if necessary. By this time, Gregório had already led his men out of the *São Paulo* and asked the crew of the *Minas* to disembark as well. The sailors on the latter ship, except for a small maintenance crew, went ashore on the 12th and the 13th. Upon reaching the naval arsenal, Cândido was immediately put in detention.[48] Interestingly, naval historian Martins argues that there was no valid reason for Cândido's arrest: his actions during the second rebellion had clearly shown he had been on the government's side—he directed the *Minas Gerais* to fire on the fort, and he refused to allow messengers from the fort aboard his ship. Cândido was accused of moving the dreadnought without orders, but there was no one to give an order, and he was acting under the threat of death by the pistol-waving radicals on his vessel.[49]

A similar denouement had taken place on the *São Paulo*. The false story of the government's massacre aboard the *Rio Grande do Sul* sent alarm through the crew, as it had on the *Minas Gerais*. But on the *São Paulo* an officer had shut down the radio transmitter, and the lack of information heightened the crew's nervousness.[50] Gregório lost control of the ships to the radicals, among whose leaders were corporal André Avelino, who had come over to the *São Paulo* from the *Deodoro* and had been second in command (*imediato*) to Gregório.[51] Gregório, like Cândido, had wanted the commander of the *São Paulo*, Silvinato de Moura, to urge Minister Leão to restore the magazines to the twelve 12-inch guns, but Silvinato had doubted the sailors' loyalty and refused to do so. The jittery crew had then grown angry, and Gregório had asked the officers to leave the ship, perhaps to save their lives, which, according to the commander, had been threatened.[52] Silvinato assented, after Gregório, apparently in control of the crew again, had agreed to maintain discipline.

On the *Bahia*, 106 crewmen left without incident on the 11th, and Dias Martins's request to leave the navy was formally implemented the same day. A few recalcitrants remained on the cruiser two more days, probably fearing reprisals ashore. On the afternoon of the 11th, Raimundo Ferreira do Vale, Commander of the *Bahia*, was appointed successor of Silvinato on the *São Paulo*, even though his ship still had disobedient sailors aboard.[53] The second in command of the *Bahia*, Lieutenant-Commander[54] Júlio César de Noronha Santos, later testified that he and his men earlier had wanted to aid the *Rio Grande do Sul* against the attempted rebellion on that ship, but "without gun magazines, without munitions of any kind, not even carbines, we decided to abandon ship."[55] On the *Deodoro*, the die-hards formed a majority of the sailors, and they held out until the 13th, four days after the uprising began.[56] After the sailors left the *Deodoro*, Corporal José Alves, who had commanded the ship during the November 22 revolt, was imprisoned for having pointed a revolver at an officer during the crisis.

The foreign press was not surprised by the second rebellion. Both *Le Temps* and the *New York Times* had predicted more instability following the November amnesty, and, when the second eruption occurred on December 9, the Parisian daily wrote that the impunity of the rebels had guaranteed a new uprising: in the interval, said *Le Temps*, some officers had refused to return to their ships under the amnesty, and sailors had not trusted the government to implement the reforms—abolishing flogging, raising the pay scale, securing better food and working conditions, and respecting the amnesty.[57]

The confusion, disorder, and insubordination occurring in the process of the disembarkation of crews in the second week of December doubtless strengthened Minister Leão's determination to ratchet up the expurgation process. He was aided by the fact that Congress, at the urging of the president, had authorized a state of siege. In the deliberations of the Chamber on that matter, opposition Deputy Irineu Machado, who had voted against amnesty in November, made the obvious point that indiscipline was provoked by the success of the first rebellion. No one rose to defend the amnesty.[58] In the Senate, only Rui Barbosa voted against the state of siege. The government declared the emergency on December 10, clearing the way of any legal barriers to official acts of repression. Edmundo Bittencourt, the editor of the respected independent daily *Correio da Manha*, said the government's suspension of civil rights would be used to accuse him, Rui, and other opposition figures of complicity in the rebellion.[59] In fact, Rui apparently went into hiding in São Paulo after the state of siege went into effect. In the interior of São Paulo, the senator from Bahia was protected by the Paulista political establishment and implicitly by the militarized state police force. At the beginning of January, Rui sent a letter to a friend in the diplomatic service regarding the relationship between the marshal and the boss of the Senate. For Rui, the president was an "imbecile beneath the spurs of that criminal [Pinheiro]. . . . The reality [of the situation] would go incalculably beyond the colors of my crayon," he wrote, referring to his predictions regarding militarism during the presidential campaign.[60] At the same time Pinheiro Machado was concerned that his enemies were playing on Hermes's *amour-propre*, suggesting to the president that he was being seen as a tool of the Riograndense senator. Pinheiro commented to Governor Borges de Medeiros in Porto Alegre, "Vanity, as you know, is a bad companion that almost always leads us astray."[61]

If the state of siege was a considerable inconvenience for Rui Barbosa, it had some justification. In the faraway state of Mato Grosso, the naval detachment operating on the Paraguay River upstream from Asunción was affected by the two rebellions, just as seamen in Amazonas in late November had been moved to plotting by the success of the first rebellion. According to the US military attaché, "On Dec. 17, the crews of the river gunboats and monitors in . . . Mato Grosso revolted, demanding more pay." They returned to duty on the 22nd.[62] The president himself later revealed that as a result of this latest mutiny, the government had "excluded," altogether, more than one thousand sailors.[63]

The policy of exclusion was effective for restoring discipline, but, unfortunately for the navy, it also created the short- and middle-term problems of recruiting and training new seamen. In May 1911, the French ambassador reported that the number of Brazilian sailors was now "notoriously insufficient."[64] The Brazilian navy resorted to hiring Portuguese nationals—presumably former sailors—to staff the ships.[65] Furthermore, a number of officers had resigned after the amnesty. The implication of all this was that in all likelihood Brazil could not adequately man its warships before Argentina received its first American-built dreadnoughts in late 1911. The US military attaché reported that after the two rebellions, "Brazil has no Navy, and in order to get one, must start all over."[66] Another result of the two revolts in such rapid succession was that Brazil scaled back its naval acquisition plan. As early as mid-December 1910, Admiral Huett Bacelar was dispatched to Britain to renegotiate Brazil's purchasing program.[67]

The government meanwhile was focused on punishment. It had imprisoned some six hundred marines and sailors by mid-December, including João Cândido.[68] Among those incarcerated was Scipião Zanotti, the *Paraíba's* radio operator, who had tipped off the rebels of government movements during the first rebellion. He was denounced in December by a fellow sailor who had alleged that Zanotti was going to lead a revolt on a submarine, on the night of December 9.[69] Thus, if João Cândido was caught by surprise when the second revolt broke out, the new rebels nevertheless seem to have tried to coordinate the mutinies of the Naval Battalion, the *Rio Grande do Sul,* and at least one other ship.

Among the hundreds of naval and marine personnel now under arrest, a group of twenty-nine men, including João Cândido and Scipião Zanotti, were sent on Christmas eve to the ancient prison in the presidio on the Ilha das Cobras.[70] The twenty-nine were dispatched to a maximum security cell that dated from colonial times and that had been carved out of rock. Tiradentes, the martyr of Brazilian independence, was said to have been a prisoner there before his execution in 1792.[71]

The cell in question had two compartments, and sixteen men were put into one, and the remaining number into the other. Each was secured by massive wooden doors, beyond which was an iron door connected to the rest of the prison. The prisoners soon exhausted the supply of fresh water, and their thirst was augmented by the stifling heat caused by the warm bodies crammed together in the small enclosure. In João Cândido's recollection decades later, the heat in the underground cell was unbearable. Still worse, it had been recently cleaned with quicklime, and as the substance dried, it was absorbed into the air that the sailors, packed together, had to breathe. Ventilation was limited to a single aperture at the top of the cell. As the water on the floor of the cell evaporated, the quicklime entered the air, and therefore the prisoners' lungs. "Clouds of lime arose from the floor and invaded our lungs, suffocating us," João Cândido later recalled.[72] The prisoners repeatedly shouted for help, but the jailor was unable to reach their cell: the commander of the fort, Marques da Rocha, had gone to the Naval Club on the Avenida Central for the Christmas holiday and had taken the key with him.

By the time the two compartments of the cell were opened on the morning of Christmas day, silence had replaced the desperate cries for help. Fourteen of the sixteen prisoners were dead in the larger group, including Zanotti, and eleven of thirteen perished in the other.[73] As in the legendary Black Hole of Calcutta, the prisoners had died of asphyxiation. The fetid air repelled the physician who was charged with certifying the cause of the deaths. Dr. Ferreira de Abreu, officially ascribed the deaths to sunstroke (*insolação*), but later changed his story, declaring the men had died of asphyxiation.[74] João Cândido must have been fit because he was one of the two who survived in the cell with sixteen prisoners.[75] Cândido and the other man, after receiving medical treatment, were returned to the same cell, which in the interim had been washed and disinfected again. Those who had died were secretly buried at night.[76]

Cândido was one of some 125 rebel prisoners who continued to suffer deprivation, including hunger, but their condition improved at the end of January 1911. In February, Dias Martins joined Cândido. The younger man had suffered similar torments after having received his discharge. The two former rebels were repeatedly interviewed by a high-ranking member of the civilian police, who sought to discover a "political" motive in the rebellion involving prominent politicians. The scandal on the Ilha das Cobras emerged slowly, and the gruesome details were only revealed by the press in February.[77] But already on December 28 the *Diário de Notícias* noted that sixteen enlisted men had just been buried, victims of "sunstroke" on the Ilha das Cobras. With grim humor, the report stated that the observatory on the Morro do Castelo, where the capital's temperature was recorded, had only registered a maximum temperature of 24.7 degrees (76.5 Fahrenheit) on Christmas, the day of the hecatomb. It was an unusually cool day for the beginning of summer. The wry and skeptical report went on to suggest that the official thermometer was no longer reliable, and that if it had been accurate, the temperature on the Ilha das Cobras would rise to much higher temperatures as summer wore on. Therefore, the article continued, all naval personnel should be withdrawn from the island to save their lives.[78]

There is considerable controversy about whether the men were deliberately suffocated. The navy denied the claim, but according to a naval historian and retired admiral, the quicklime could be introduced through the small air hole at the top of the cell as a riot control device: it "dried . . . [the prisoners'] throats, making impossible their shouts of suffering or of revolt." In his 1998 book on naval prisons, Admiral Juvenal Greenhalgh even supplies a photograph of the aperture in the ceiling of a maximum security cell in the island's prison, implying that such cells still exist, possibly including the one where Cândido's fellow prisoners died![79]

President Hermes duly ordered an investigation of the responsibility of the fort's commander, Francisco Marques da Rocha, who was relieved of his duties on December 28. The investigating board was headed by Pereira Leite, the former commander of the *Minas Gerais*. Marques was exonerated, and later the president even invited him to dinner at Catete Palace.[80] Marques da Rocha was eventually promoted to *Capitão de Mar e Guerra*, the same rank that the martyred commander of the *Minas Gerais* had held.

João Cândido remained in prison in the early months of 1911. In this period, he asked his jailor for newspapers, a fact that makes clear that he was literate. But at the same time he suffered delirium. He frequently could "see and hear" his dead companions. For a time he was sent to an infirmary in Copacabana, where he would have seascape panoramas to distract him from his terrors. That procedure apparently failed to have the desired effect, so on April 18 a naval medical board sent him to the national insane asylum (Hospital Nacional de Alienados), located in Urca, a district abutting Botafogo and across the water from Flamengo. During his enforced idleness Cândido got another patient to record his "memories," which he titled "The Life of João Cândido, or the Dream of Liberty."[81] When his condition improved in early June, Cândido was again sent to the naval prison on the Ilha das Cobras.[82] For months, he remained in isolation from the other prisoners.

A punishment equal in its barbarity to the asphyxiation scandal, involving far larger numbers, was to begin on that same Christmas day on which Cândido's cell mates expired. This second event was the dispatch of hundreds of prisoners—men from the navy and marines, and men and women from the prisons, jails, and streets of Rio de Janeiro—to the uppermost reaches of the Amazon Valley, in newly acquired Acre. There were precedents for such an indiscriminant roundup of radicals, beggars, prostitutes, and vagabonds: In 1905 President Rodrigues Alves's minister of justice, J. J. Seabra, had forcibly transported lower-class participants in the 1904 riots to the Amazon. Such punishment was Brazil's version of Siberian exile—which would be formalized in 1924 with the opening of a prison camp called Clevelândia, adjacent to French Guiana. Purging the city of "undesirables" had become a Carioca institution.[83]

The man who supervised the roundup and Amazonian exile of lower-class Cariocas in December 1910 was José Antonio Flores da Cunha, the inspecting *delegado auxiliar* of the Federal District, "delegado" being a kind of plenipotentiary prosecutor of the capital's police force. Flores, from the county of Livramento on the Rio Grande-Uruguay border, was a protégé of Pinheiro Machado. He was ruthless, brave, hotheaded, and politically ambitious.[84] Two years after the events described here, Pinheiro promoted Flores da Cunha to Congress, where he was assigned to represent Ceará, a northeastern state in which he had never set foot.

The *Satélite*, the makeshift prison ship leaving Rio on Christmas Day 1910, was a vessel in the national merchant marine, Lloyd Brasileiro. Its journey to Acre—the territory that Rio Branco had wrested from Bolivia in 1903—was recorded in detail by the ship's captain, Carlos Brandão Storry, in his report to the company in March 1911.[85] The ship had boarded 105 men discharged from the navy, 202 vagabonds, and forty-four women (presumably prostitutes), guarded by fifty soldiers led by three second lieutenants. Because a stoker of the *Satélite* was ill on Christmas day, Captain Storry recruited one of the prisoners to fill that role. According to Storry, this man, José Pedro da Rocha, immediately denounced a plot for a prisoner revolt, to take place at midnight on the 25th-26th. It would be led by Hernâni Pereira dos Santos, known as "Sete" (Seven). The soldiers thereupon forced the sailors accused by the stoker into the hold of the ship, while they conducted a military inquiry amounting to a kangaroo court. The accuser asserted that Sete would be assisted in the revolt by Aristides Pereira—the "Chaminé" who had urinated on the corpse of the martyred captain of the *Minas Gerais*. Vitalino José Ferreira, the killer of a naval officer on November 22, was also named as a conspirator.[86] According to the stoker, the military officers in charge of the ship's prisoners were all to be killed. The three officers decided the allegations were true. At 11 p.m. that night, they had Sete shot and his body thrown into the sea. Others were handcuffed and 128 more soldiers boarded at Recife, Pernambuco, on December 31. The following day four more prisoners were executed and Chaminé "jumped" overboard, while handcuffed.[87]

The remaining prisoners on the ship were all forced below deck, not to see daylight again for weeks. They arrived at Santo Antônio on the Madeira River, a tributary of the Amazon, on February 2. On the following day the military detachment charged with the construction of telegraph lines in the Amazon Valley received two hundred men from the *Satélite*.[88] The line crews, part of a widely publicized state-building project that may have had as much to do with appearances as reality, had made a two-month journey from the Rio de la Plata up the Paraguay River, through Mato Grosso and thence to Acre. They were led by the legendary Colonel Cândido Rondon, who would found Brazil's Indian Protection Service in 1912 and would lead Theodore Roosevelt down the River of Doubt the following year.[89]

Those still left on the ship were supposedly destined for work on the Madeira-Mámore Railroad, part of Rio Branco's geopolitical strategy to tie Acre firmly to Brazil, as well as to compensate Bolivia for its territorial loss. The railhead was only seven kilometers from Santo Antônio at Porto Velho, but the American builders there refused to let the prisoners disembark, perhaps because of their ill health.[90] In any event, tropical diseases took a huge death toll on the workers who constructed the rail line.[91] So the remaining male prisoners were delivered to rubber-tapping contractors who needed laborers. The women were disembarked at Santo Antônio to serve as prostitutes in the rubber-tapper camps.

Captain Storry's narrative tells us a little about the prisoners he had transported in a list he presented to Lloyd Brasileiro. Some had notations after their names, such as "dangerous brawler" or "dangerous robber." For many of the men, and more of the women, Storry had recorded only their given names, such as João Manuel, Maria Inácia, or Catarina "so-and-so" (*Catarina de tal*). Beginning the journey back to Rio on the same day the prisoners were all disembarked, Storry recorded that he and his crew left Santo Antônio, "free and safe from the clutches of such perverse bandits." Presumably he was referring to the prisoners, not the soldiers.[92] The ship returned to Rio on March 4, 1911.

Another eyewitness to the agony of the prisoners, Booz Belfort de Oliveira, worked for the sanitary service of the government telegraph commission. He contacted Rui Barbosa in May 1911 and charged that as many as ten prisoners had been shot on the *Satélite*, in addition to the one thrown into the sea alive. He and other telegraph personnel from Colonel Rondon's mission entered the *Satélite*, and Belfort affirmed that the prisoners were packed below deck "like sardines in a can." These men and women, who had not seen light for forty-one days, on February 2 were brought out under the blazing Amazonian sun. They were "dying of hunger, bony and nude, reminiscent of the old slave compounds," wrote Belfort. Still another Rondon Commission member used similar words.[93] The rags they wore revealed their whole bodies, and the women had only shirts to wear. The rubber contractors chose the strongest-looking men, after Lt. Matos Costa had taken two hundred of them for service on the telegraph lines. Because the women, all of whom were distributed for prostitution, were in poor health, Belfort thought none might still have been alive at the time he wrote in May 1911.[94]

The men who were to help lay the telegraph lines fared as badly. They had to sleep on the ground with no cover, subject to malaria. In the construction of the lines, they had to do the most brutish jobs, in a temperature of at least 39 degrees celsius (102 fahrenheit) in the shade, receiving little food. Not surprisingly, they finally despaired. According to Belfort, Lt. Matos Costa personally executed two with his pistol. Another was shot dead with a rifle, on February 18, "to serve as an example," wrote Belfort.[95] Later, however, a plot against the soldiers was hatched by "marinheiro" (sailor), who one historian thinks was almost certainly a survivor of the Naval Battalion revolt.[96] At all events, Rondon, whose team laid nearly 2,300 kilometers of telegraph lines in Mato Grosso and Amazonas in the years 1907–15, employed corporal punishment to keep his workers in line, despite the termination of that practice in the army in 1874 and in the navy in 1910.[97]

The *Satélite* scandal, like that of the asphyxiation of João Cândido's cellmates, brought Rui Barbosa's wrath down on Hermes. Rui not only publicized and denounced the two atrocities when the *Satélite* scandal was revealed in May 1911, but he returned to the outrage of the *Satélite* at the beginning of the administration of Hermes's successor, Venceslau Brás. In December 1914 the senator from Bahia alleged that the proof of the crimes could be found in the national archives as well as in those of the ministries. Or more precisely, if justice hadn't been done, it was because the federal government suppressed the documents that proved its complicity: Hermes was "the most responsible" of those implicated. His ministers of justice and the navy had tried to cover up the crime,[98] and the former had organized the *Satélite* massacre with funds supplied by the navy, claimed Rui.[99]

João Cândido counted himself lucky for not having been sent north on the *Satélite*, though his own punishment was almost fatal. In retrospect, he thought he had been left off the list of the *Satélite*'s "passenger" list because of the intervention of Pinheiro Machado.[100] But the sailors still in the hands of the navy—João Cândido foremost among them—had to face yet another ordeal. It was a military trial to determine whether the men who had been amnestied in November were culpable in the Naval Battalion revolt the following month. A Council of Inquiry interviewed forty witnesses regarding the behavior of seventy-six sailors who had participated in the events of December 9–12. But only thirteen of the seamen under investigation gave statements: the others had fled, or had already been sent to their native states.[101] Those remaining were tried for improper conduct before a formal court-martial (the Conselho de Guerra). The indictment, read in June 1912, alleged that "the defendant João Cândido, leader of the first movement, from which he gained great prestige among his companions, used that prestige to maintain indiscipline [during the second revolt], . . . sending radiograms to the government . . . ordering cannon fire, and arming the crew of the ship [*Minas Gerais*]." Others named specifically with charges of disobeying orders included Francisco Dias Martins, Manuel Gregório de Nascimento, and Ernesto Roberto dos Santos, who had killed a sergeant loyal to Commander Neves.[102]

The attorneys for the defense included Evaristo de Morais, the most famous criminal lawyer of the day. Morais, who had been an abolitionist, was also a labor lawyer, defending the rights of dockworkers (most of whom were black). He, Jerônimo de Carvalho—himself partly of African ancestry—and Cícero Monteiro de Barros had been contracted by the Brotherhood of Our Lady of the Rosary, an organization established in Rio in 1640 and dedicated to the welfare of blacks.[103] Not all the defendants before the court-martial were Afro-Brazilians, however.[104] The lawyers undertook the case on a pro bono basis.[105] Instead of making full depositions, the defendants, to the extent possible, let their lawyers answer the prosecution. Carvalho, Morais, and Monteiro argued that their clients were not guilty because they had not violated the amnesty they received. The court-martial concluded that in the rebellion of the Naval Battalion in December 1910—the one for which the sailors were being tried—João Cândido and his mates had been loyal to the government, and that he had reported to Commander Pereira Leite, not communicating with the Naval Battalion rebels.[106] He had moved the *Minas Gerais* without orders to do so, but he had done so to load coal for the attack on the Ilha das Cobras and to get out of range of rebel fire. Credible witnesses backed João Cândido's testimony and that of the other men accused. The naval officers who composed the jury of the court-martial announced their verdict on December 2, 1912, and unanimously absolved the defendants, even Ernesto Roberto dos Santos, who had killed Sgt. Francisco de Albuquerque, and Vitorino Nicássio, who had dispatched Lt. Claudio da Silva. The two victims had tried to defend Commander Batista Neves on the night of November 22. The court not only acknowledged that Cândido and the others had defended the government during the second uprising, but that the infractions of the naval code they committed were simple disciplinary matters, not under the jurisdiction of the court-martial.[107]

§5 Past and Present

What did the naval revolt of November 1910 mean? There were many answers. Inevitably, the dramatic events of the "Revolt of the Whip," as it came to be called, in which lower-class sailors, the majority of them Afro-Brazilians, overpowered their white officers and demonstrated their sailing skills, would call into question convictions about the social order, citizenship, and Brazil's role in the community of nations. A central issue was race and its relationship to Brazilian nationality.

Out front in the controversy were Brazil's literary figures, who shared a trait with their counterparts in nineteenth-century Russia: both groups were also the leading social critics of their day. Writers like João do Rio, Lima Barreto, and Sílvio Romero criticized the social and political worlds in which their literary creations moved.[1] All the same, unlike many members of the Russian intelligentsia, Brazilian intellectuals were reformists rather than revolutionaries.

The opening salvo in the controversy about the relationship between the revolts, race, and Brazilian society, however, came from the anonymous "Officer of the Navy."[2] His angry book was titled *Politics versus the Navy*,[3] and the author found fault with President Hermes and the political establishment, the navy as an institution, and the sailors who had revolted. He considered Hermes's decision to pass the issue of the rebellion on to Congress an act of cowardice. For the anonymous writer, the navy had in no way prepared its officers and men for their responsibilities with the new dreadnoughts and other modern warships. "We are the navy of Haiti," wrote "Officer." He had especially harsh words for the black sailors, who were in chronic ill health and exhibited "all the depressing signs of the most backward African peoples," including sloth and rowdiness. To control such a group, the lash "was literally indispensable," wrote the anonymous critic.[4] But he also wanted fewer officers, a lower retirement age for them, and new technical training for both officers and men. "No one in the navy, from the highest to the lowest, has practical occupational training," he wrote. Numerous observers of the seamen's handling of the ships on November 23–26 would have disagreed. "Officer" does concede that the men of the Brazilian lower deck were aware of their rights, but contrasts the respect the British seamen show to their officers with that of the Brazilians.[5] The anonymous critic of the navy nonetheless expressed hope that the "regenerated nation" could overcome the problems of backward races. Regeneration would occur under the guidance of a moralizing military dictatorship, an idea in line with the views of reformist army officers.[6] During the Hermes administration these violence-prone soldiers wanted to overthrow the dominant regional oligarchies in state governments.

The race prejudice of "Officer" was shared by the martyred commander of the *Minas Gerais*, Batista das Neves. Loading coal on the ship's maiden voyage had been "very sluggish," Neves complained, because "the people engaged in it were all blacks [*gente de cor preta*], exhibiting the indolence . . . of that race."[7] Some foreign visitors had a similar low regard for Afro-Brazilians. Georges Clemenceau, who had been the French premier in 1907–9 and would again lead his country during the last years of World War I, had visited Brazil in September 1910 and had spoken at Rio's new Teatro Municipal exactly two months before the Revolt of the Whip erupted. Though he was not in the Brazilian capital during the November and December rebellions, in *Notes on a Voyage to South America*, Clemenceau ventured that the successive uprisings were "principally due to the impulsiveness of African blood."[8]

Thus the undisguised race prejudice of "Officer" was hardly unique. But his book was polemical enough to provoke a response from Álvaro Bomílcar, a literary figure and journalist from Ceará. Like "Officer," Bomílcar was a resident of Rio and a white. In a series of newspaper articles published in 1911 that he collected into a book five years later, Bomílcar admitted that the "naval question" was a difficult one, but one to which race prejudice posed a great obstacle to a solution.[9] In fact, race prejudice was "the true cause" of the uprisings in November and December 1910.

In this short work, Bomílcar holds that race prejudice is totally without justification, because of the nonexistence of meaningful racial differences between black and white. There is, he wrote, no such thing as a pure race. Like his contemporary Sílvio Romero, Bomílcar identified the Brazilian "ideal type" as having equal measures of black, white, and Amerindian ancestors. Racism was an "aesthetic necessity of an ultra-ridiculous aristocracy [from which naval officers were drawn] in a democratic republic."[10] Bomílcar idealized race relations in the army, holding that the most worthy soldiers could rise to high rank "without distinction of color and caste." But naval officers had to be members of the solid bourgeoisie and be "as white as possible." If João Cândido had enjoyed the education of the ordinary naval officer, "he would have doubtless been a good ship commander." Bomílcar's reform of the navy would have allowed the best students in the naval apprentice schools to attend the naval academy and would have required all cadets to spend at least a year in the ranks before entering the academy.[11]

Bomílcar ends his book with an appeal to modern science and calls Jean Finot, a French historian, the outstanding authority on race. Finot, citing a large literature in French, English, and German in his study *Race Prejudice*, examines the arguments for racial stratification—anthropological, psychological, cultural, and historical—and finds them all baseless. "In one word, the term race is only a product of our mental activities, the work of our intellect, and outside all reality. . . . Races as irreducible categories only exist as fictions in our brains," proclaimed Finot.[12] "All human races are equal in mental capacity," affirmed Bomílcar, echoing Finot.[13]

Other issues were imbricated with race. That many officers despised the rebels resulted not only from the class and racial chasms between officers and men, but also the alleged practice of homosexual acts by the sailors. In 1911 the Liga Marítima Brasileira condemned promiscuity in the ranks: this attribute, the Liga contented, was part of their base character.[14] If "honor" was violated by homosexual acts, most officers probably believed that ordinary soldiers or sailors had no honor to lose. "But . . . enlisted men did not agree," in the words of a historian of the common soldier. "For the most part they accepted and upheld as best they could the code of honor common to civilian society."[15] Of course, the fact that crews traveling overseas had to spend weeks or months together without female companionship might give rise to homosexual practices, but in that regard the Brazilian navy would hardly have been unique. In fact, the navy's attitude toward homosexual acts was more liberal than one might suspect. The naval penal code of 1891 punished sodomy with one to four years of prison *only* if force was involved, or if the act was perpetrated against a minor.[16] Adolfo Caminha's novel of 1895, *Bom-Crioulo*, cited above for its reference to savage flogging, is built around a homosexual relationship between a muscular black sailor—a former slave—and a blue-eyed cabin boy from southern Brazil. In *Bom-Crioulo*, however, Caminha refers to the same-sex orientation of some of his fellow officers, as well as of their men.[17] In any event, homosexual activity was a source of opprobrium in Brazilian society, and homosexuals such as João do Rio had to hide their sexual orientation. But that writer's career, including membership in the Academy of Letters, illustrates that discreet gay men, including those of mixed race, were not excluded from Brazil's highest honors.

During the First Republic, the religious condemnation of sodomy as a sin was being replaced by a "medicalized" interpretation of homosexuality as an illness. Sodomy was not a criminal act under the Brazilian criminal code of 1890. In fact, sodomy had been decriminalized in the Code of 1830.[18] Brazilian physicians had a scientific interest in sodomy and other aspects of homosexual behavior. Dr. José Pires de Almeida made a study of homosexuality in 1906, surveying ancient and modern history, but focusing on Brazil in the late empire and early republic. He cites the work of the Austrian Richard Krafft-Ebing and other authorities of his day and sees homosexuality as deviant behavior, in some cases of a hereditary nature.[19] Noting homosexual practices in boarding schools, Pires writes that naval vessels present similar situations. Long voyages oblige men to enter into "deviant forms of sexual love. Repetition of such necessary acts, which initially are endured with disgust, finally provides pleasurable satisfaction."[20]

Did the men of the 1910 revolt engage in homosexual acts? There is no proof, although Belo, the first naval officer charged with writing a "corporate" history from the navy's perspective and hardly an unbiased observer, refers to João Cândido's unspecified "problem of a moral order" for which he should not have been allowed to reenlist in 1905.[21] We do have some ambiguous indications of João Cândido's love life. During his recuperation from the ordeal of Christmas eve 1910, at the prison on the Ilha das Cobras, the traumatized sailor found solace in embroidering, a pastime that may have been related to sewing skills developed in his previous work as topman. In charge of the main mast, Cândido had had to work with complicated cords that moved the sails, and from there embroidery was not a distant leap.[22] The themes of two surviving pieces of his embroidery are enigmatic. One is called "Amor," showing a bleeding heart pierced by a sword. The other surviving piece of embroidery includes the names of Francisco Dias Martins and João Cândido, but the historian Carvalho believes that "amor" might refer to a relationship Cândido had with a cabin boy or younger sailor, possibly the one with whom he appears in several newspaper photos in November 1910, reminiscent of the novel *Bom-Crioulo*.[23] The sociologist Gilberto Freyre writes that NCOs often had homosexual relations with the young sailors they protected.[24] In any event, all this is necessarily speculation.

Sexuality was not the only matter on which race, class, and notions of honor were intertwined. An issue in which race loomed large was what the Revolt of the Whip indicated about the Brazilian political process and, indeed, the character of the Brazilian people. Writing in the wake of the bombardment of the Ilha das Cobras in mid-December 1910, the literary and social critic Sílvio Romero wrote that the mutineers were violent braggarts who had revolted, slaughtered officers, bombed the capital city, and threatened to destroy it. The federal Congress caved in to the threat, bowing to Pinheiro Machado, as if he were president—"the lord who wouldn't take no for an answer on this, his ranch." In the history of humanity, "there was no other example of three or four hundred black sailors—or almost black, most of them—who have defeated a nation."[25] He goes on to condemn the political oligarchy that presided over the disgrace and to bemoan the absence of civic culture in Brazil. Romero lamented that Brazil was ruled by caudillos, of which Senator Pinheiro Machado was the most powerful and egregious example. Romero saw Pinheiro as a "submissive servant to the tendencies of the masses" who, like other caudillos, "think they are in control of this poor land and this unfortunate people." The boss of the Senate was "surely the most detestable political boss that Brazil has had the misfortune to count [among its rulers]."[26]

Whether education was the solution Romero envisioned in his diatribe remains unclear, but he has no doubt that Brazil had suffered international humiliation in the (allegedly black) sailors' revolt. Consistency was not his forte, and Romero's views had shifted significantly since 1888, when, as a professor at Recife, one of Brazil's two law schools, he wrote that "every Brazilian is a *mestiço*, if not by blood, in his ideas." At the time, he saw in racial hybridity the possibility of "national viability."[27] This, in sharp contrast to the views of Raimundo Nina Rodrigues, professor of legal medicine at the medical school of Bahia. Rodrigues considered Afro-Brazilians "an impediment to white civilization, or better put, one of the elements in our inferiority as a people."[28]

It was precisely in the decade 1910 to 1920 that the issue of national character was being reassessed, as Brazilian intellectuals tried to come to grips with the fact that a huge fraction of the national population was not predominantly white, in contrast with Argentina's immigrant-fueled Europeanization. Alberto Torres's two influential essays, *The Brazilian National Problem* and *National Organization*,[29] were both published in 1914, and the pace of the debate quickened with intellectuals' partial rejection of European models of civilization as the old continent tore itself apart in 1914–18.[30]

Some contemporaries and later commentators agreed that Brazilian statesmen and the public at large had confused the symbols of modernity—in this case the two great battleships—with the substance, which was the result of a long-term and complex process of modernization involving changes in education, economic structures, and inevitably, social structures as well. Ambassador Lacombe had written to the Quai d'Orsay of the Brazilian elite's desire "to appear" modern. Father Louis Gaffre, another contemporary French observer who had been in Rio at the time of the second revolt, put it well: Brazil's mistake, he wrote, lay in its "intense desire to place itself at the same level as that of the great civilized nations; its capital error had been to [try to] skip stages" of development.[31] "Officer" had pointed out that neither the majority of the naval officers nor their men had been adequately instructed. This was also the opinion of Naval Minister Leão at the time, and that of the sociologist Freyre a half-century later. Freyre wrote that the majority of the naval officers were not properly trained for the new navy, but had been educated in traditional humanities like the attorneys coming out of the two leading law schools in São Paulo and Recife: they were "arts-and-letters officers [*oficiais bacharelescos*]" wrote Freyre in 1959.[32]

The navy's corporate memory of the Revolt of the Whip, which naval officers refer to as the Sailors' Revolt, is evidenced in a number of accounts by participants in the events—notably Pereira da Cunha and Bello, in his unfinished history of the rebellion. Pereira thought sailors regarded flogging as a test of manhood.[33] In the view of historian Arias Neto, Pereira da Cunha perfects the argument of the anonymous letter by "Ex-sailor."[34] The "deifiers" of João Cândido had confused his ability to pilot the ship in the bay (*governar*) with navigation. For Pereira, the former required no great skill.

Furthermore, since fewer than half of the sailors of the squadron had revolted, argued Pereira da Cunha, it couldn't properly be called a revolt of the sailors. The rising hadn't been a revolt, but was a *motim*—a tumult, a riot, a row. Emphasizing the savagery of the rising, Pereira denies that João Cândido was the leader of the movement, based on the letter by "Ex-sailor," who credits Dias Martins with the leadership. Implicitly Dias Martins emerges as white, an inference that I have argued that is far from proven. In addition, for Pereira da Cunha, the revolt was a boon for the navy because it resulted in Decree 8400, which allowed the service to dismiss sailors without formal procedures.[35]

Yet there was also another corporate memory in the navy—that of the sailors. In the decades following the Revolt of the Whip, various discontented and potentially revolutionary groups harkened back to that event. In December 1915, a plot of some one hundred army sergeants was discovered, and many were forced to retire. A second conspiracy of noncoms was discovered the following April. *Correio da Manhã* reported that Deputy Maurício de Lacerda, a lawyer who defended anarchists, was conspiring with Francisco Dias Martins, elements in the Naval Batallion, labor militants, and active duty NCOs in the army. The NCOs wanted to protect their careers and obtain social and political reforms, including the right of suffrage. Had the plot succeeded, the sailors excluded in 1910 would also have been reincorporated into the armed forces. But it came to nought, and according to the newspaper, former sailors "roamed the docks of the port, dressed in rags."[36]

The memory of the Revolt of the Whip surfaced again in 1935. Brazil, like a number of European nations, had become increasingly polarized in the first half of the 1930s as the Brazilian Communist Party and the (fascist) Brazilian Integralist Action both expanded rapidly. The Communists, led by Luís Carlos Prestes, a former army officer with an almost mythic past of revolutionary action, attempted a coup d'état against the dictator-turned-legal president, Getúlio Vargas, in November 1935. A flyer by "a group of Liberating Sailors" appealed to fellow seamen to take revolutionary action. ("Liberating" referred to the Alliance of National Liberation, the leftist coalition organized by the Communist Party.) Just as João Cândido's revolt had ended flogging in the navy, the document asserted, the sailors of 1935 should overthrow Vargas, the agent of foreign imperialists. But the revolt was quickly crushed. About the same time, Benedito Paulo published his short book on the naval revolt of 1910—the first such undertaking, viewing the sailors as heroes, later betrayed by the government.[37]

The most serious movement to arise in the ranks of the navy occurred
in 1964, in the run-up to the military coup of March 31 of that year. Again,
Brazilian politics was growing increasingly polarized, as the government
of João Goulart began to enact land-reform measures and to threaten the
profits of foreign investors. Meanwhile peasant leagues were organizing
in the Northeast and the consciousness-raising mass literacy movement
of Paulo Freire threatened traditional social relations in the both city and
countryside. A memoir by Avelino Bioen Capitani, a sailor who participated in the resistance against the coup and subsequently joined a guerrilla movement against the military dictatorship, asserts that "the history
of the Revolt of the Whip was engraved in the memory of the sailors"
of his generation. "It was one of the first stories that they told me in the
barracks," he wrote. In 1962 a group of enlisted men founded the Association of Sailors and Marines to defend the corporate interests of the two
groups. Capitani wrote that for a second time in a half-century—the first
being in 1910—sailors had organized themselves against the general staff
of the navy. An assembly of the association, drawing some forty-five hundred enlisted men, denounced physical abuses of sailors and demanded
that the navy recognize their organization as legitimate. Militant seamen
resisted in March 1964, but their ancient rifles were no match for those of
the army. The memorialist Capitani was tortured before escaping to Cuba
for training in guerrilla warfare.[38]

A week before the coup, the president of the enlisted men's association
had compared João Cândido and his companions to their successors in
the 1960s. Just as the former had abolished whipping, so the present-day
seamen would abolish the "moral flogging" by which sailors were denied
the right to vote and other civic rights.[39] In fact, the sailors got João Cândido to speak at one of their meetings, though he offered something less
than a ringing endorsement: "I didn't expect to witness another revolt
[in my lifetime], but I have the impression that you, too, are tempting
fate."[40] He was right; repression followed quickly and the military would
rule the country for two decades.

Exeunt Omnes

The dreadnoughts: The giant warships, *Minas Gerais*, *São Paulo*, and
Rio de Janeiro, whose acquisition fueled the dreams of power of Foreign
Minister Rio Branco and the Brazilian admiralty, each met a different

fate. In both world wars Brazil was a belligerent, but the *Minas* and the *São Paulo* fought in neither. Brazil declared war on Germany in 1917, and the sister ships were assigned to the Allies' Grand Fleet. They were in poor condition, however, and their refitting outlasted the war. In the 1930s the Brazilian navy replaced the original guns on the *Minas* with new cannon and substituted oil-burning boilers for coal-fired ones. But when Brazil again went to war with Germany in 1942, the ship was only deployed in coastal waters to protect the port of Salvador. It was sold for scrap in 1954. A worse lot befell the *São Paulo*: it was in sorrier condition than the *Minas* by the 1930s and was not judged worthy of modernization. During World War II it served as a floating battery off the port of Recife. Sold for scrap in 1951 and towed to Europe, during a storm off the Azores it broke tow and sank without a trace. Its precise location remains a mystery.

The largest of the Brazilian dreadnoughts, the *Rio de Janeiro*, still building at the time of the Revolt of the Whip, saw action in World War I, but not under Brazilian colors. Doubts about the wisdom of completing the battleship had risen sharply after the 1910 revolt, and the collapse of Brazil's rubber boom in the face of Asian competition helped make financing the *Rio de Janeiro* impossible. In December 1913, Brazil sold the ship to the Ottoman Empire for £2,750,000, that is, £250,000 less than she had paid. The huge vessel, now rechristened *Sultan Osman I*, was completed in August 1914, just as the world war broke out. Winston Churchill, then first lord the admiralty, seized the ship, fearing that Turkey would ally with Germany in the conflict then raging. Churchill's action, in fact, probably contributed to the Ottoman decision to join the Central Powers. The huge dreadnought, having "the greatest number of turrets and heavy guns ever mounted on a battleship,"[41] now became the *Agincourt*, named for Henry V's victory over the French army in 1415. The *Agincourt* participated in the Battle of Jutland in May 1916, only to be decommissioned three years later. The Royal Navy then attempted to resell her to the original owner, but bitter experience was a good teacher, and this time the Brazilian government rejected British blandishments. The *Agincourt* was scrapped in 1924, three decades before the *Minas Gerais* and the *São Paulo* met their end. All in all, Brazil's experience with the great ships had brought neither power nor glory.

The actors: For the remainder of Hermes da Fonseca's mandate, Pinheiro Machado maneuvered for control of the government, having as his chief rivals the army officers who had ousted the traditional elites in

Northeast Brazil, now calling themselves *salvacionistas*. Of these, the most important was General Dantas Barreto, the first minister of war in the Hermes administration. The president was meanwhile distracted. His wife had died in 1912, and he married again while in office. As Hermes became increasingly absorbed in attending to his beautiful new bride, Nair de Teffé, Pinheiro got the upper hand and effectively ruled the country in the marshal's final year of office, 1914.[42] The senator's influence declined with the inauguration of President Venceslau Brás in November of that year. Pinheiro's scorn for the populace remained intact, and five years after the naval rebellion, he was stabbed to death by an unemployed baker from his home state at a fashionable hotel in Rio. No chief of state or prime minister of Brazil has ever been assassinated, and Pinheiro Machado was probably the most powerful Brazilian politician ever to suffer that fate.[43]

The baron of Rio Branco found himself at odds with President Hermes in late 1911 because of trouble brewing in Bahia, the state where the baron's family had originated. The "salvations" of state governments by army officers involved violence, and as at Manaus in 1910, in January 1912, the army bombed Salvador, Bahia's capital, to oust the governor. This outrage caused Naval Minister Leão to resign his post.[44] It was also a source of embarrassment verging on mortification for Rio Branco, who had always striven to portray his country as one ruled by law. Threatening to resign, he persuaded Hermes to restore the incumbent governor of Bahia to power. But the baron had serious kidney problems exacerbated by his irregular and excessive eating habits, and he died in February.[45]

Hermes da Fonseca left office in November 1914 and the following year was elected to one of the three Senate seats of Rio Grande do Sul. He did not take office, however, because of the assassination of his friend Pinheiro Machado. Hermes then withdrew from Brazilian politics and spent six years in Switzerland. In 1921 he returned to Brazil and was elected president of the Military Club; it had once again become an important institution in the political process, as it had been in the last years of the empire. In the contested election of 1922—the only such event between 1910 and 1930—the former chief of state got involved in an abortive attempt to keep president-elect Artur Bernardes from taking power. Hermes went to prison for six months and died in 1923. During his lifetime he became known as the *urucubaca*, a term from the Afro-Brazilian cult of macumba signifying "bewitched," because of the events associated with his own bad luck and that of those around him.[46]

After 1910, Rui Barbosa continued to play an important role in Brazilian politics. He ran for president in the following election, but abandoned the campaign after Minas Gerais and São Paulo joined forces again to support Hermes's vice president, Venceslau Brás. Rui entered the lists for the presidency once more in the special election of 1919, but was defeated by the northeasterner Epitácio Pessoa, who enjoyed the support of Minas, São Paulo, and Rio Grande do Sul. The senator from Bahia declined to represent Brazil at the Versailles Peace Conference, yet in 1921 he accepted a permanent seat on the World Court at the Hague, where he had gained an international reputation at the Peace Conference of 1907. He died in Brazil in 1922.

The lives of the principal rebels after 1910, with the exception of João Cândido himself, are largely obscure. Francisco Dias Martins was involved in the sergeants' conspiracy of 1916, and at an unrecorded date he sailed to French Guiana and subsequently to France. He returned to his native state of Ceará and may have died in Fortaleza, but little is known of his later life.[47]

Of Manuel Gregório de Nascimento, we know that soon after his acquittal, he applied for employment with President Hermes.[48] Perhaps surprisingly, the rebel sailor was given a job in the garage of Catete Palace and later moved to the pantry. Forgiveness was part of the patron-client system. In the 1930s, according to João Cândido, Gregório became a government agent and worked for the secret police during Getúlio Vargas's Estado Novo dictatorship (1937–45).[49]

In the years following the acquittal of João Cândido Felisberto, according to his own account, the navy got him fired from jobs in the Brazilian merchant marine. He received occasional favors from his former patron, Senator Pinheiro Machado, who even invited him to dine in his home on the Morro da Graça—but only in the kitchen![50] He traveled to Argentina and then to Greece on a Greek ship. The chronology of his travels is unclear, but Cândido was back in Rio at the time of the Spanish influenza in 1918. He settled down as a fisherman and fishmonger at the market on Praça XV de Novembro sometime between 1919 and 1922. Cândido thereafter remained in the fish market, in the heart of the city, cheek-to-jowl with the Naval Ministry and the Ilha das Cobras. He raised a family in the suburban lower-class town of São João de Meriti in the Baixada Fluminense. The former sailor outlived two wives and married a third, only ceasing to work in 1960 at the age of eighty.[51]

As a symbol of black and lower-class resistance, João Cândido's stature grew with time. The populist governor of Rio Grande do Sul, Leonel Brizola, awarded him a modest pension in 1959. But the military coup of 1964 emboldened his successor, an opponent of Brizola, to cancel the subsidy.[52] João Cândido Felisberto expired on December 6, 1969, at the age of eighty-nine. He had suffered from lung cancer and was survived by his third wife and several children. As the Revolt of the Whip receded in time, new honors arrived. In 2001 a bust of the deceased sailor was erected in a public park in Porto Alegre, the capital of Rio Grande do Sul. Seven years later Brazilian President Luís Inácio Lula da Silva signed Law no. 11,756, offering posthumous amnesty to the mutineers of the Revolt of the Whip, confirming the amnesty of November 25, 1910.[53]

Although the bust in Porto Alegre was put on display at the beginning of the new millennium, naval opposition to honoring the rebel sailor succeeded in blocking any memorial in Rio de Janeiro until 2007. At that time a statue was erected on the grounds of the former presidential residence, Catete Palace, where Hermes da Fonseca had resided. The statue, now seen by some as a symbol of Brazil's aspiration for racial equality, was moved to Praça XV and reinaugurated in the presence of President Lula on November 20, 2008. The monument shows João Cândido facing the open bay, where the Revolt of the Whip took place, with his right hand on a ship's pilot wheel. The inscription beneath the bronze memorial relates that João Cândido Felisberto "led the Sailors' Revolt against the deplorable working conditions and flogging [that in theory had been] abolished in the Golden Law of 1888," freeing the slaves.[54] This official statement could be interpreted as a celebration of resistance by the lower classes as much as by blacks alone. Perhaps it was meant to be ambiguous. That the inscription used the term "Sailors' Revolt" rather than "Revolt of the Whip" may have been a concession to the navy. In any event, as the centenary commemoration approached, the conferences, publications, films, and debates about the mutiny made abundantly clear that "history" had not forgotten the Revolt of the Whip, as Rio Branco had hoped, even if Brazilians disagree on its meaning and moral import.

Notes

Preface

1. A famous fictional account of a slave rebellion aboard ship is Herman Melville's *Benito Cereno*, a novella based on an actual uprising on a Spanish slaver recounted by Amasa Delano, in his *Narrative*, vol. 1, chap. 18.

2. Allen, *Port Chicago Mutiny*, 64–65 and 72.

Chapter 1

1. Dantas Barreto, *Expedição*, 220.

2. Lima Barreto, *Recordações*, 136.

3. The term "Cidade Maravilhosa" was coined by the writer Henrique Coelho Neto in 1908, but it gained international fame with the 1934 Carnival march by André Filho.

4. Solis and Ribeiro, "O Rio," 56.

5. E. da Silva, *As Queixas*, 86–87.

6. Lima Barreto, *Gonzaga de Sá*, quoted in Machado, *Lima Barreto*, 153.

7. On the architecture of the Avenida Central buildings, see Needell, *Tropical Belle Epoque*, 40–44.

8. J. C. Rodrigues, *João do Rio*, 100. On Rio's beautification in these years, see Costa and Schwarcz, *1890–1914*, passim.

9. Ferrez, "Avenida," 29.

10. O Clube Naval, *Clube Naval*, n.p.

11. Needell, *Tropical Belle Epoque*, 44.

12. Maestri, *Cisnes*, 13.

13. Enders, *Histoire*, 241; Costa and Schwarcz, *1890–1914*, 90.

14. The first Pan American Conference was held Washington, DC, in 1889, and the second, in Mexico City in 1901; Buenos Aires hosted the fourth meeting in 1910.

15. Named for US President James Monroe, whose name was associated with Pan Americanism.

16. In subsequent years the building served a variety of state functions, most notably housing the Brazilian Senate from 1923 to 1960. The structure was demolished by the military government in 1976.

17. See the photographs in Brazil, Directoria Geral de Estatística, *Boletim*.

18. Romero, *Estudos sociaes*, 55. Brazil had no universities as such until the twentieth century, and the "doutores" were graduates of medical, law, and engineering schools.

19. Scott, *Seeing Like a State*, 130.

20. J. M. Carvalho, *Bestializados*, 93.

21. Named for their style of fighting, deploying foot blows. Capoeira became ritualized into a graceful dance, set to rhythmic music, with near-misses of feigned kicks between "combatants."

22. E. da Silva, *As Queixas*, 122.

23. Medeiros, *Os indesejáveis*, 38. This policy continued into the interwar period, when local authorities tried to channel most of the prostitution into the Mangue (swamp) district, where the practice was fitfully regulated. See Caulfield, "Birth of Mangue."

24. The following year the police force of the capital was put under the direct jurisdiction of the minister of justice.

25. Needell, "Revolta," 247. The Jacobins were radical nationalists and xenophobes who had considered themselves the heirs of Floriano Peixoto, the authoritarian marshal who defended Rio against naval rebels, monarchists, and foreign powers in the civil war of 1893–95. They vigorously and sometimes violently opposed his civilian successor, Prudente de Morais. Their influence as an organized group withered quickly after the failed attempt on Prudente's life in 1897. On Jacobinism, its ideology and social foundations, see Queiroz, *Radicais*.

26. J. M. Carvalho, *Bestializados*, 117. An obvious hypothesis would connect the riot to the demolition of slum housing, but Carvalho underscores the challenge to civil rights posed by the government's attempt to make smallpox vaccinations obligatory. Orators denouncing the campaign emphasized the invasion of households and the threat to citizens' virtuous wives and daughters. That is, they claimed that the vaccination decree violated the individual liberty and personal honor of fathers and husbands. Carvalho points out that the two redoubts of the revolt, the districts of Saúde and Sacramento, were not significantly affected by the urban renewal. J. M. Carvalho, *Bestializados*, 130, 136. On the sweep of the city in 1904 by Minister Seabra, also see Meade, "Civilizing," 114.

27. Of 811,000 in 1906. Medeiros, *Os indesejáveis*, 63.

28. Ibid., chapter entitled "Anarquistas e comunistas," 93–125.

29. Ibid., 274.

30. Bretas, *A guerra*, 62.

31. J. M. Carvalho, *Bestializados*, 86. My figures, from the Directoria do Serviço de Estado, differ slightly from Carvalho's. See Brazil, Directoria Geral de Estatística, *Estatística*, 244–45.

32. J. M. Carvalho, *Bestializados*, 86. He notes that in New York City, during the presidential election of 1888, 88 percent of the adult male populated voted, and in Rio, during the presidential contest of 1896, only 7.5 percent did so.

33. Ambassador Lacombe, cited in Capanema, "Nous, marins," 71.

34. Rio, *A alma*.

35. Ibid., passim (Joaquim mentioned on p. 35). The historian Eduardo da Silva also mentions this practice, indicating that Joaquim was not unique, in *As Queixas*, 76.

36. Most notably, Chagas disease, identified in 1909 by Carlos Chagas. On Cruz and his institute, see Stepan, *Beginnings*, passim.

37. Morgan, "Legacy," 165.

38. Martins Filho, *A marinha brasileira*, 34; Magalhães, *Rui*, 218.

39. Magalhães, *Rui*, 248–66, 389–419.

40. Classic Encyclopedia, "Baron Adolf Von Marschall Von Bieberstein."

41. Tuchman, *Proud Tower*, 284.

42. However, the law was not effectively implemented for another ten years.

43. Beattie, *Tribute*, 209.

44. An epic struggle memorialized by Euclides da Cunha in *Os Sertões* (1902), translated as *The Backlands* (2009). For an interpretation of the events in question, see Levine, *Vale of Tears*, passim.

45. Fonseca Filho, *Marechal Hermes*, 77, 124.

46. During the First Republic, the only enduring political organizations were the Republican Parties of each of the states.

47. Chargé Lacombe to Minister Stephen Pichon, quoted in Capanema, "La construction," 68. This was by no means a uniquely Brazilian characteristic: note Amuchástegui's description of the Argentine *farolero* in *Mentalidades*, chap. 1.

48. As noted above, the politically conscious and active members of Brazilian society were a small minority of the Brazilian people: the Constitution of 1891 had granted the franchise only to literate male citizens twenty-one and older, and only 2 to 3 percent of the country's total population actually cast votes in the presidential elections from 1894 through 1910. Apathy, in the face of violence, intimidation, and systematic fraud, was a logical result of the Brazilian system of *coronelismo* (rural bossism).

49. Love, *Rio Grande do Sul*, 146.

50. A naval officer in the events described below, Pereira da Cunha, thought sailors had been affected by Rui's campaign. Maestri, *Cisnes*, 22.

51. On Pinheiro's domination of the president and the corrupt practices of the PRC, see Love, *Rio Grande do Sul*, 147, 149–52.

52. Love, *Rio Grande do Sul*, 143.

53. Mantua, *Figurões*, 157.

54. Pronounced "gaoo'shoos."

55. Ibid., 177.

56. Ibid., 157, 166.

57. Amado, *Mocidade*, 127.

58. Mantua, *Figurões*, 176. The standard form was "seu."

59. Amado, *Mocidade*, 128.

60. The notion of the decisive nature of naval power in the struggle for empire was given a boost in the United States and elsewhere by Captain Alfred Thayer Mahan's book, *The Influence of Sea Power Upon History, 1660–1783* (1890). The most important chapters were translated and published in the Brazilian navy's *Revista Marítima Brasileira*. Martins Filho, *A marinha brasileira*, 40–41.

61. The Japanese army also defeated its Russian counterpart decisively at the battle of Mukden.

62. The rise in US power in the region was evident from 1895, when Grover Cleveland successfully insisted on arbitration of the British Guiana-Venezuela boundary dispute.

63. In fact, the US Navy had asserted its power in Brazilian waters in 1894, when it broke a rebel blockade of the port of Rio de Janeiro. At the time US Admiral Andrew Benham commanded the largest squadron in Guanabara Bay. Topik, *Trade*, 148.

64. Keegan, *First World War*, 258–59.

65. The new canal was completed in 1914.

66. *Encyclopedia Britannica*, vol. 14, 311.

67. Brazil's first president, a marshal of the army, had increasingly found himself at odds with the civilian-led congress in a period of economic recession. In November 1891, he dissolved Congress, an illegal act, and touched off a rebellion by civilian and naval opponents, forcing Deodoro's resignation on Nov. 23, and his replacement by the vice president, Marshal Floriano Peixoto.

68. Arias Neto, "Em busca da cidadania," 219–23.

69. Brazil, Ministério da Marinha [Min. Júlio César da Noronha], *Relatório*, 1904, 4.

70. According to Souza e Silva, *Assumptos navaes*, 13.

71. Brazil, Ministério da Marinha [Min. Júlio César da Noronha], *Relatório*, 1905, 7.

72. Decree of 24, Nov. 1906. Also see entry on "Ship" in *Encyclopedia Britannica*, vol. 14, 906. This article identifies Brazil as the initiator of the South American naval race.

73. Capanema, "Nous, marins," 70.

74. Souza e Silva, *Assumptos navaes*, 1, n. 1. An earlier booster of naval preparedness was the journalist Arthur Dias, author of *O problema naval* (1899).

75. Ibid., 26, 30, 93. France would have six battleships, but Souza argued that their quality was lower than that of the Brazilian ships.

76. Information in this paragraph from ibid., 1, n. 1, 26, 30, 93–94.

77. Like the United States, Brazil named its largest capital ships after its states.

78. Martins Filho, *A marinha brasileira*, 138.

79. The *São Paulo* was built in the Vickers shipyards at Barrow-in-Furness and was completed in July 1910.

80. "Nominal radius 10,000 at 10 knots." Jane, *Jane's Fighting Ships*, 435. But the *Encyclopedia Britannica* says eight thousand nautical miles, vol. 14, 906. The difference might be accounted for by the presumed speed at which the ship was moving.

81. Lambuth, "Naval Comedy," 1432.

82. Calculated from data in Ludwig, *Brazil*, 355.

83. Capitão de Mar e Guerra.

84. Plus others, notably his second-in-command, Lieutenant-Captain Americano Freire, his artillery chief, and his turret commander. Souza e Silva, *Assumptos navaes*, 161–62.

85. Ibid., 151, 154, 156, 162.

86. Hough, *Potemkin*, 70.

87. *Encyclopedia Britannica*, vol. 14, 906. Jane, *Jane's Fighting Ships*, 435.

88. Martins Filho, *A marinha brasileira*, 123.

89. Ibid., 84, 128.

90. Lacurte, "Lotação," Arquivo da Marinha.

91. *The Times*, Mar. 3, 1911, 7.

92. *Encyclopedia Britannica*, vol. 14, 906. The pound was equivalent to US$4.86 in 1910.

93. Souza e Silva, *Assumptos navaes*, 172.

94. Ibid., 206.

95. Martins Filho, *A marinha brasileira*, 158–59.

96. *Encyclopedia Britannica*, vol. 14, 906.

97. On these matters, see Scheina, *Latin America*, passim.

98. Rio, *A alma*, 92–93.

99. Austria-Hungary, largely landlocked, had a naval base on the Adriatic, near Trieste.

100. Amado, *Mocidade*, 54.

101. "Navios de Guerra Brasileiros: 1822–hoje"; Poder Naval & Marítimo. "Bem-Vindo ao Poder Naval Online."

102. Souza e Silva, *Assumptos navaes*, 220.

103. But see below on racial composition of the lower ranks.

104. Bomílcar, *O preconceito*, 28.

105. See Evaristo de Moraes Filho, "Prefácio," in E. Morel, *A revolta*, 3d ed., 12, where he says the navy drew its officers from the elite, while the army tended to get its leaders from the middle class. Also see J. M. Carvalho, "Forças armadas," 224, and H. L. Martins in interview with S. Capanema, on Aug. 9, 2006, in which he states that naval officers were "very much linked to the aristocracy." Capanema, "Nous, marins," 544.

106. Nascimento, "Do convés," 101.

107. On his race, see Nascimento, *Cidadania*, 111.

108. Zachary Morgan thinks that sailors were darker than Brazil's soldiers and Brazilian society on the whole. Morgan, "Legacy," 6.

109. At the end of the empire the term "pardo" was used for all children of former slaves who had been born free, though generally "pardo" meant of mixed black and white ancestry. On these issues, see Capanema, "Nous, marins," 159–65.

110. Capanema, "Etre Noir," 6–7. In Brazilian censuses, classifications varied as well from one census taker to the next.

111. Morgan found that, of the 344 sailors tried for crimes in Rio de Janeiro in 1860–94, only 14.8 percent were white, and 8.1 percent were of unstated color. The rest were various shades of black or brown—that is, partly or wholly of African descent. (Figure includes 13.7 percent *caboclo*.) Morgan, "Legacy," 77. Nascimento found a similar racial composition in the 13th company [circa 1910?]. Omitting men of unknown color, of 52 men, he found 40 percent *pardos* (mixed), 29 percent *pretos* (blacks), 25 percent white, 4 percent *caboclos*, and 2 percent mulattoes. Therefore, the large majority were black or brown. Nascimento, "Do convés," 61. Even if one classifies the *caboclos* with the whites, in both studies the large majority remain African-derived in whole or part.

112. His book had no date of publication, but it was circulating in Brazil in 1911.

113. Oficial da Armada, *Política*, 85.

114. Morgan, "Legacy," 22.

115. Leão, *Relatório*, 32. On the uses of recruitment in the army, see Beattie, "Conflicting Penal Codes." Alvares Barata, "Revolta," 108.

116. Morgan, "Legacy," 149; Arias Neto, "Em busca da cidadania," 246; Maestri, *Cisnes*, 26.

117. Law 4901 of July 22, 1903 as in Brazil, Ministério da Marinha [Júlio César da Noronha], *Relatório*, 47.

118. Arias Neto, "Em busca da cidadania," 50.

119. Oficial da Armada [José Eduardo de Macedo Soares], *Política*, 90. Brazil, Leão, *Relatório*, 20.

120. Capanema, "Modernização," 10, on training programs. See below on the Bureau of Naval Identification.

Chapter 2

1. *The Economist,* June 5, 6, and 19, 1909, 1178–79, 1283, 1314, 1359.

2. Antônio Eduardo Villaça to Conde de Salir, June 25, 1910, Arquivo do Ministério de Negócios Estrangeiros. (He cites *Correio da Manhã,* Rio, May 22, 1910.)

3. Capitão de Fragata Carlos Pereira Lima, report on voyage, Correspondence, SDM, July 2, 1910, as cited in Capanema, "Nous, marins," 15, n. 61. (Capitão de Fragata was the rank just below Capitão-de-Mar-e-Guerra.)

4. *O Século,* Oct. 1, 1910, 1; *O Mundo,* Oct. 1, 1910, 1; *O Mundo,* Oct. 2, 1910, 1.

5. *O Mundo,* Oct. 3, 1910, 1.

6. *A Luta,* Oct. 4, 1910, 1.

7. Based on Fonseca Filho, *Marechal Hermes,* 128–29.

8. Serrão and Oliveira Marques, *Nova História,* 697–98. On the role of sailors, see also newspaper accounts cited in following note.

9. *O Século,* Oct. 5, 1910, 1; *O Mundo,* Oct. 5, 1910, 2; *A Luta,* Oct. 5, 1910, 1–2.

10. *O Século,* Oct. 5, 1910, 1.

11. *A Luta,* Oct. 4, 1910; Oct. 1 and 7, 1910, 1.

12. The ship would see action in Mozambique against the German navy in 1916.

13. *O País,* Nov. 23, 1910, 1.

14. Fonseca Hermes had reversed the name of his father, also named Hermes da Fonseca, to distinguish himself from his brother.

15. *O País,* Nov. 23, 1910, 4.

16. Dantas Barreto, *Conspirações,* 163.

17. Maestri, *Cisnes,* 75.

18. Dantas Barreto, *Conspirações,* 171–72.

19. Capitão-de-Mar e Guerra.

20. Chargé Lacombe to Stephen Pichon, Nov. 28, 1910. Martins, "A revolta," 104.

21. Aristides Pereira, nicknamed "Chimney." Ibid., 114.

22. Ibid., 104, 114; Cândido, "Memórias," Jan. 7, 1913; E. Morel, *A revolta,* 3d ed., 79. Flying a red flag was customary in naval rebellions, but it is possible that it could also have been associated with the red standards displayed in the 1904 revolt against compulsory vaccination, directed in part by socialist and positivist radicals. On the flag in 1904, see Needell, "Revolta," 238.

23. Bello, "Elementos," 9.

24. Bryce, *South America,* 396. Bryce had been a member of Parliament and minister in several Liberal governments. He was the author of numerous works on foreign affairs, the best known of which was *The American Commonwealth* (1888).

25. That he made himself scarce in the early moments of the rebellion is confirmed in his "Memórias," Jan. 6, 1913.

26. But Bello seeks to minimize the role of João Cândido, as against that of Francisco Dias Martins. "Elementos," 9.

27. Cândido, *Memórias*, Jan. 7, 1911, 1. But Bello claims Cândido's secretary was Durval Seixas. "Elementos," 9.

28. Bello, "Elementos," 9.

29. Dantas Barreto, *Expedição*, 173.

30. J. C. Carvalho, *O livro*, 322. "Commander" is equivalent to Capitão-de-Mar-e-Guerra.

31. Martins, "A revolta," 115.

32. José Alves da Silva, who had commanded the *Deodoro*, was also only twenty at the time of the revolt. Morgan, "Legacy," 234.

33. "Ex-marinheiro," 20, Arquivo Nacional. Maestri, *Cisnes*, 72.

34. Martins, "A revolta," 116.

35. Crew members of the *República* later boarded the larger rebel ships. Martins Filho, *A marinha brasileira*, 188.

36. Ibid., 115, 118, 120. Maestri, *Cisnes*, 74.

37. Morgan, "Legacy," 222.

38. Ibid.; for the numbers of officers and crews for 1909, see Arias Neto, "Em busca da cidadania," 252.

39. Martins, "A revolta," 118.

40. The Brazilian navy was behind the times in this respect because the unification of officers' careers—engineers and combatants—in the US Navy had already begun in 1897. Martins Filho, *A marinha brasileira*, 175.

41. Ibid., 131–32.

42. This was Matias Bitencourt Carvalho. E. Morel, *A revolta*, 3d. ed., 73.

43. Freyre, *Ordem*, vol. 1, cxxvi.

44. US Office of Naval Intelligence. Register 799, 4. Ambassador Bryce agreed that Britons were forced to operate engines, *South America*, 396. Martins, "A revolta," 128.

45. Morgan, "Legacy," 190.

46. On "admiral" and deaths, see Cândido, "Memórias," Jan. 7, 1913. Cândido denied that he or other sailors had donned officers' uniforms. Rather, he wore a red silk kerchief around his neck, "Memórias," Jan. 8, 1913.

47. Maestri, *Cisnes*, 74.

48. J. C. Carvalho, *O livro*, 321.

49. Cândido, "Memórias," Jan. 7, 1913.

50. Named for the sixteenth-century French naval captain who founded "Antarctic France" in Brazil.

51. The minister of war, Dantas Barreto, notes this fact in a memoir, but he doesn't say why the forts were silent. *Conspirações*, 172.

52. Martins, "A revolta," 124.

53. "Ex-marinheiro," 17, Arquivo Nacional.

54. J. C. Carvalho, *O livro*, 321.

55. Named for the date of the proclamation of the republic, Nov. 15, 1889.

56. Cândido, "Memórias," Jan. 7, 1913. Cândido doesn't say what the role of the *Bahia* was.

57. J. C. Carvalho, *O livro*, 328, 331.

58. Ibid., 341.

59. The two verified deaths were of children. Castelo Hill was demolished in 1921.

60. Martins, "A revolta," 123.

61. J. C. Carvalho, *O livro*, 341.

62. Martins, "A revolta," 123.

63. *O País*, Nov. 23, 1910, 1.

64. The "Memorial" incorrectly attributed the title of senator to Carvalho.

65. See facsimile of text in Martins, "A revolta," 111–12.

66. Capanema, "Nous, marins," 224. Maestri, *Cisnes*, 23.

67. Batista das Neves, Relatório of May 2, 1910, cited in Capanema, "Nous, marins," 195.

68. Bello, "Elementos," 8.

69. Lacurte, "Lotacão," Arquivo da Marinha. On size of crew at time of revolt see J. C. Carvalho, *O livro*, 320.

70. Martins Filho, *A marinha brasileira*, 181.

71. See below.

72. Freyre, *Ordem*, vol. 2, 736. Oficial da Armada, *Política*, 78.

73. According to an informed but anonymous British observer, João Cândido, leader of the rebellion and veteran seaman first class, earned only fifteen pounds sterling a year. Extract from unsigned letter by British officer who witnessed the rebellion, from chargé d´affaires ad interim in Buenos Aires, Dec. 19, 1910, 2. Copy found in Dudley to Secretary, Dec. 19, 1910, US National Archives.

74. *Diário de Notícias*, Nov. 24, 1910, 1.

75. E. Morel, *A revolta*, 5th ed., 339; Martins, "A revolta," 133; Bello, "Suscintos elementos," 10.

76. *Correio de Manhã*, Nov. 24, 1910, 2.

77. See Nascimento, "Do convés," 25.

78. First Lieutenant Milcíades Portela Alves, who saw other officers killed on the *Minas Gerais*, wrote that he prayed for a second revolt in which the amnestied sailors would revolt again. Reproduced in Pereira da Cunha, *A revolta da esquadra*, 70–75, and in a more widely accessible version in Braga, *1910*, 381–87.

79. Martins, "A revolta," 124.

80. Arias Neto, "Em busca da cidadania," 266.

81. On the torpedo problems, see Brazil, Leão, *Relatório*, 7–9; Martins, "A revolta," 128; Arias Neto, "Em busca da cidadania," 267.

82. Imperial and Foreign Intelligence, "The Mutineers and the President," [British] National Archives.

83. Martins, "A revolta," 128.

84. Ibid., 128–29.

85. Capitão-de-Mar-e-Guerra.

86. J. C. Carvalho, *O livro*, 347; Martins, "A revolta," 149–50.

87. *Correio da Manhã* said, "It is . . . verified, by the laments of the revolting men, that the meals offered in the sailors' mess halls are pernicious, prepared with adulterated and rotten produce, not suitable for dogs," Nov. 26, 1910, 1. Morgan's translation, *Legacy*, 212. João Cândido was quoted in the *Diário de Notícias* on November 24 that sailors' food was "scant and of the worst sort" (péssima e pouca).

88. J. C. Carvalho, *O livro*, 255.

89. Cf. the townspeople of Fuenteovejuna in Lope de Vega's play of that name (1619). When asked who had killed the Crown's agent, they replied, "Fuenteovejuna, Señor." Responsibility was collective.

90. J. C. Carvalho, *O livro*, 357.

91. Martins, "A revolta," 151–52.

92. Dantas Barreto, *Conspirações*, 178; J. C. Carvalho, *O livro*, 364; Martins, "A revolta," 152.

93. Martins, "A revolta," 124.

94. Capanema, "Nous, marins," 297.

95. Cândido, "Memórias," Jan. 8, 1913.

96. Brazil, Congresso Nacional, *Annaes do Senado Federal*, Nov. 24, 1910, 128.

97. Ibid., 134.

98. Ibid., 135.

99. Ibid., 137.

100. Arias Neto, "Em busca da cidadania," 271–72.

101. Brazil, Congresso Nacional, 137.

102. Arias Neto, "Em busca da cidadania," 271–72.

103. Brazil, Congresso Nacional, 137–38. The senators representing São Paulo were Francisco Glicério, Alfredo Ellis, and former president Manuel Campos Sales.

104. Romero and Guimarães, *Estudos sociais*, 27. See above on Pinheiro Machado's education.

105. Brazil, Congresso Nacional, 139.

106. Ibid., 142.

107. Ibid.

108. Ibid., 143.

109. Ibid.

110. Ibid., 142.

111. Ibid., 145.

112. Ibid., 146.

113. Ibid., 146–47, 150.

114. Ibid., 156–57.

115. See Arias Neto, "Em busca da cidadania," 269. Morel thinks the telegram brought back by Carvalho was forged, as does Maestri, *Cisnes*, 85, but H. L. Martins thinks it might be authentic, "A revolta," 221. On the general issue of possibly faked telegrams in the crisis, see Morgan, "Legacy," 238.

116. J. C. Carvalho, *O livro*, 367.

117. Capitão-de-Fragata.

118. Cândido, "Memórias," Jan. 2, 1913.

119. National Maritime Museum, "Research Guide."

120. Admiral Jorge Dodsworth Martins, "Memórias," Arquivo da Marinha. Martins, "A revolta," 129. It is interesting that Cândido, in his "Memórias," Jan. 5, 1913, refers to the 1797 revolts as an example of what seamen could accomplish. It is possible that he learned of the British revolts after November 1910; Rui Barbosa gave details of the events in England in his speech against the state of siege in December. Or perhaps João do Rio, the editor of the *Diário de Notícias*, inserted this observation in Cândido's memoirs. Braga, *1910*, 337; J. C. Rodrigues, *João do Rio*, 157–60.

121. Imperial and Foreign Intelligence, Nov. 24, 1910, The National Archives.

122. Topik, *Trade*, 148–49, 154.

123. Dudley to Division, Nov. 23, 1910, National Archives.

124. *O Malho*, Dec. 3, 1910, n.p. Maestri, *Cisnes*, 79.

125. This is E. Morel's opinion, *A revolta*, 3d ed., 88.

126. Leão, Untitled order to sink rebel ships, Nov. 25, 1910, Arquivo da Marinha.

127. Martins, "A revolta," 125–26. Martins doubts that the message had been written by ordinary seamen, because of the formal style in which it was written.

128. *O País*, Nov. 27, 1910, 1. Martins, "A revolta," 125–26. "Health and Fraternity" (*saúde e fraternidade*) was a mistranslation of "Salut et Fraternité" (Greetings and Fraternity), a slogan of the French Revolution. But the former phrase was the greeting adopted by the Brazilian Republicans in 1889.

129. Reported in *Jornal do Comércio*, Nov. 26, 1910, 2.

130. Martins, "A revolta," 129.

131. *O País*, Nov. 25, 1910, 3. This edition refers to events on the 25th, so it was published the same day. Also see Martins, "A revolta," 162. To the extent that the government forged telegrams, "reclamantes" would have been preferred to "os marinheiros revoltosos."

132. *O País*, Nov. 25, 1910, 3. This demand arrived in a separate message from the other sent on the 25th.

133. See below.

134. Maestri, *Cisnes*, 88.

135. Bello, "Suscintos Elementos," 11; Maestri, *Cisnes*, 87.

136. Capanema, "Nous, marins," 300.

137. Capitão-de-Mar-e-Guerra.

138. Cândido, "Memórias," Jan. 8, 1913, 1.

139. According to one account, sailors on the *Deodoro* opposed the acceptance of the amnesty. They prepared a statement saying the president of the republic and the Minister of the Navy should have come aboard, and that salaries should have been raised. They blamed João Cândido for not insisting on these items, but they finally agreed to surrender the ship. One other source, an interview in 1946 with Marcelino Rodrigues, the sailor whose scourging had ignited the rebellion, supports this interpretation. However, no later historian makes any claim about the disagreement among the crews. See Paulo [Pereira Nunes], *A revolta*, 47–48, for the allegation, and Marcelino Rodrigues interview, *O Globo*, Oct. 4, 1946, for support. But see Arias Neto, "Em busca da cidadania," 274 and 293, who dismisses Paulo as unreliable.

140. Dantas Barreto, *Conspiracões*, 178, 189.

141. Brazil, Congresso Nacional, 170.

Chapter 3

1. Arias Neto, "Em busca da cidadania," 50.

2. For text of decree, see ibid., 175.

3. Cf. Bom Crioulo, in the novel of the same name: he reflects that "a sailor and a black slave—in the long run, they come down to the same thing." Caminha, *Bom-Crioulo*, 80.

4. For example, Oficial da Armada, 89.

5. [Adm.] Alvares Barata, "Revolta," 106. See also the demonstration of his indifference to pain expressed by Bom Crioulo during his savage whipping of 150 strokes. Caminha, *Bom-Crioulo*, 35. But this is only the perception of the officer who wrote the novel.

6. *Diário de Notícias*, Nov. 29, 1910, 1; Cândido, "Depoimento," 71. "Ex-marinheiro," Arquivo Nacional. I infer that this anonymous writer is none other than Francisco Dias Martins, although such identification is controversial. My view is based on a comparison of the handwriting in the account of Ex-sailor (Ex-marinheiro) with a signature of Dias Martins I found in a police report. Marcelino Rodrigues, whose brutal whipping had sparked the revolt, thought that Dias had died in 1946, but he didn't claim direct knowledge of the Cearense's death. Bello, however, thinks Dias lived another forty years after

1910. See "Inquérito," Arquivo Nacional; Interview with Marcelino Rodrigues, *O Globo*, Oct. 4, 1952; Bello, "Suscintos Elementos," 12.

7. Martins, "A revolta," 134.

8. "Ex-marinheiro," Arquivo Nacional, 9–10, 12. On the Bahia's stop in Buenos Aires, see US Office of Naval Intelligence, "Mutiny," US National Archives.

9. "Ex-marinheiro," Arquivo Nacional, 14. This was also Bello's opinion. "Elementos," 7.

10. E. Morel, *A revolta*, 3d ed., 44; Kagan, *Peloponnesian War*, 440.

11. Bello, "Suscintos Elementos," 1. Bello, who as a young naval lieutenant had served the government during the revolt, also wrote another version of these matters, "Elementos autênticos." As a retired naval officer charged with composing an official account of the events, he may have had the advantage of access to documents no one else has seen, with the exception of H. L. Martins. The latter took over the assignment after Bello died.

12. Alencar had been minister of the navy under Presidents Afonso Pena and Nilo Peçanha. He was to be interim minister under Hermes da Fonseca, and minister once again under President Venceslau Brás.

13. Cândido, "Depoimento," 76.

14. That is, kept him off the death ship, the *Satélite* (see Chapter 4). Cândido, "Depoimento," 82. When Pinheiro became Cândido's patron is not clear, but the relationship may date back to the war of 1893–95, when Pinheiro led irregular troops for the governments of President Floriano Peixoto and Governor Júlio de Castilhos. According to his own account, João Cândido, though still a child, fought under Pinheiro's command. Cândido, "Memórias," reproduced in E. Morel, *A revolta*, 5th ed., 291.

15. J. M. Carvalho, "Os Bordados," 74. For reference to signalman see Cândido's official record book, "Caderneta," 348 b, Arquivo Nacional.

16. Martins, "A revolta," 137. Cândido, "Depoimento," 87, 99. "Caderneta," 345A,353A,354A. The record book would have listed any floggings and did list other forms of punishment.

17. Ibid., 346A, 350B3, 354B , 355A

18. "Caderneta," 347B.

19. Ibid., 355A. Cândido, "Memórias," Jan. 1, 1913, 1; Cândido, "Depoimento," 78–79. Cândido stated that the German navy allowed him, as helmsman of the *Benjamim Constant*, to bring the ship through the Kiel Canal in 1906 [sic] "governando o navio."

20. Bello, "Suscintos elementos," 3.

21. Ibid., 4.

22. "Caderneta," 354B. In 1909 Cândido didn't get to play Neptune, because of a wound he received from another sailor. Martins, "A revolta," 136.

23. In the novel *Bom-Crioulo*, written by a naval officer, the modern battle-

ship was a "redoubtable steel prison . . . whose code of discipline—a horribly heavy work-load—didn't allow him [the black protagonist] to go ashore every second day, as was customary on the other ships." Caminha, *Bom-Crioulo*, 89. On "conegaço," see Arias Neto, "Em busca da cidadania," 343. Cf. Freyre's term "cônego," in *Ordem*, cxxvi.

24. Especially by Gregório and the Bahiano André Avelino de Santana. Bello, "Suscintos elementos," 7.

25. Capanema, "Nous, marins," 207.

26. Other leaders, according to João Cândido's own account, were the telegrapher Ricardo Freitas, who had joint responsibility on the *Bahia* with Dias Martins, and André Avelino on the *Deodoro*. See E. Morel, *A revolta*, 5th ed., 74.

27. João Cândido implies that he did take part in the planning, but doesn't say so directly in his "Memórias," Jan. 5, 1913.

28. Bello, "Suscintos elementos," 7.

29. His title was *mestre d'armas*. João Cândido notes that several musicians were involved in the conspiracy. "Memórias," Jan. 5, 1913. Perhaps their involvement indicates their greater degree of literacy, assuming that if they could read musical notation, they were also literate. Literacy would also afford them a broader political consciousness than that of illiterate sailors.

30. Capanema, "Nous, marins," 346.

31. Conselho de Guerra, Nov. 30, 1912, Arquivo Nacional.

32. José Alves, "commander" of the *Deodoro*, and assisted by André Avelino, was also twenty years old. Morgan, "Legacy," 20.

33. The fact that Dias Martins' mother had had to work her way to Rio to be present for his trial in 1912 lends credence to the view that he was unlikely to have had a secondary education. See *Gazeta de Notícias*, Dec. 31, 1912, 1. "Ex-marinheiro," 2. See also Martins, "A revolta," 136.

34. *Gazeta de Notícias*, Dec. 31, 1912, 1. "Ex-marinheiro," 1–4. Moreover, João Cândido could read, as shown by his request for newspapers while in prison.

35. Conselho de Guerra, Nov. 30, 1912, 697A-701A.

36. Martins, "A revolta," 133. The children of Adalberto Ferreira Ribas claimed that their father had been the author of the manifesto, but their account is faulty on other matters of fact, and I find their testimony, ninety-nine years after the rebellion, not credible. Although there is no dossier for Adalberto in the GIB archive, Sílvia Capanema notes that he had a good education (*culture letrée*), but his brother Beda appears in the GIB records as only having a "primitive" (*rude*) level of instruction. See GIB registro no. 155. Consult Capanema, "Nous, marins," 345 and 355, for a different view on Adalberto Ribas's role in the revolt. (Capanema, "Nous, marins," 536, confirms that Adalberto had a brother named Beda.)

37. Interview with Marcelino Rodrigues, *O Globo*, Oct. 4, 1952 (clipping supplied by Marco Morel).

38. "Ex-marinheiro," 14, 17.

39. The first to do so was probably Heitor Pereira da Cunha, who had been chief of staff to Naval Minister Leão. Pereira da Cunha, *A revolta da esquadra,* 27.

40. Ibid., 1.

41. *Careta,* Dec. 3, 1910, 3.

42. Conselho da Guerra, Nov. 30, 1912. Annexos ao processo do Conselho de Invés. das praças envolvidos nos acontecimentos posteriores a anistia . . . Rio, Oct. 2, 1911, 809.

43. Capanema, "Nos, marins," 154–56, 158; Capanema, "Modernização," 7.

44. Capanema, "Nos, marins," 156.

45. For example, to be used in the trial to which the rebels of November 1910 were subjected.

46. Capanema, "Nos, marins," 158.

47. *Jornal do Brasil,* Nov. 25, 1910, 1; in all, twenty sailors had died, according to Maestri, *Cisnes,* 74.

48. *O País,* Nov. 24, 1910, 1: "A Revolta dos Marinheiros."

49. Martins, "A revolta," 157.

50. *FonFon,* Dec. 3, 1910.

51. *Careta,* Dec. 10, 1910.

52. Amado, *Mocidade,* 56.

53. Lima Barreto, *Recordações,* 1.

54. *Le Figaro,* Nov. 25, 1910, 2; Nov. 26, 1910, 2; *Le Temps,* Nov. 26, 1910, 1; *O Século* (Lisbon), Nov. 25, 1910 (quoting the *Times* of London).

55. *Le Temps,* Nov. 26, 1910, 1; *New York Times,* Nov. 26, 1910, 3: "Surrendered to the Mutineers"; Bryce, *South America,* 396. The French chargé d'affaires also thought the rebellion was nonpolitical, Lacombe to Pichon, Nov. 28, 1910.

56. *New York Times,* Nov. 26, 1910, 3; *Outlook,* Dec. 10, 1910, 800.

57. *Le Figaro,* Nov. 25, 1910, 2; and Nov. 26, 1910 2.

58. *New York Times,* Nov. 28, 1910, 3; Dec. 6, 1910, 11.

59. "Patriote Bresilien" in *Le Matin,* cited in *La Vie Maritime,* Dec. 10, 1910, 641; *Gil Blas,* Nov. 28, 1910: "Les origines et les causes des troubles au Brésil."

60. *Le Temps,* Nov. 26, 1910, 1; Lambuth, "Naval Comedy," *The Independent,* Dec. 22, 1910, 1431.

61. *The Spectator,* Dec. 3, 1910, 954.

62. *Le Temps,* Nov. 26, 1910, 1; *Outlook,* Dec. 10, 1910, 800; *The Spectator,* Dec. 3, 1910, 954.

63. *Le Temps,* Nov. 26, 1910, 1; *Outlook,* Dec. 10, 1910, 800; *The Spectator,* Dec. 3, 1910, 954; *The Nation,* Nov. 26, 1910, 354.

64. Oficial da Armada, 93–94.

65. *Current Literature,* Jan. 1911, 31.

66. *New York Times,* Nov. 26, 1910, 3: "Surrendered to the Mutineers."

67. Dudley to Secretary of State, US National Archives. The expert handling of the ships also gave rise to the suspicion among Brazilian leaders that officers might have been involved. M. Silva, 60.

68. *Le Figaro*, Nov. 25, 1910, 2.

69. *Current Literature*, Jan. 1911, 31.

70. US Office of Naval Intelligence, Lt. John S. Hammond, "Brazilian Naval Revolt, 1910," US National Archives.

71. *Collier's*, Jan. 7, 1911, section 1, 19.

72. Martins, "A revolta," 158; Pereira da Cunha, *A revolta da esquadra*,, 40.

73. *La Prensa*, Nov. 24, 1910, 11; Nov. 25, 1910, 10–11; Nov. 26, 1910, 13; and Nov. 27, 1910, 12.

74. US Office of Naval Intelligence, Lt. John S. Hammond, "Brazilian Naval Revolt, 1910," 5–6. US National Archives.

75. "Ex-marinheiro," 12, 13, Arquivo Nacional.

76. *Jornal do Comércio*, Dec. 6, 1910, signed by its author on Dec. 2.

77. Pereira da Cunha, *A revolta da esquadra*, 98. Cf. the fact that in the parliamentary debate on the abolition the public use of the lash on slaves in 1886, defenders of slavery argued that such whipping was absolutely essential for controlling their bondsmen. Otoni, *Autobiografia*, 274–75.

78. Oficial da Armada, *Política*, 89.

79. Alvares Barata, 106.

80. See above, and Cândido, "Memórias," Jan. 5, 1913. Capt. Durão Coelho says seven men, so Cãndido exaggerates.

81. "Ex-marinheiro," 7.

82. Cândido, "Memórias," Jan. 5, 1913.

83. Capanema, "Nous, marins," 328.

84. *Careta*, Dec. 3, 1910, n.p.

85. For example, Bryce, *South America*, 396. Also see Martins, "A revolta," 133.

86. Capanema, "Nous, marins," 194.

87. Cf. the protagonist of Adolfo Caminha's *Bom-Crioulo* (Good darkie). Written by a naval officer in 1895, the book is set in the period when the Brazilian navy was shifting from wind-powered ships to steam-powered steel ships, and the author mentions the difficulty of the protagonist in adapting to the new technology. Caminha, *Bom-Crioulo*, 79, 89.

88. Martins, "A revolta," 137.

89. Ibid., 137; Arias Neto, "Em busca da cidadania," 343.

90. Martins, "A revolta," 131–32.

91. Carew, *Lower Deck*, 25–27.

92. Brazil, Leão, *Relatorio*, 23. A naval officer writing forty years later, Admiral Antão Alvares Barata, specifically mentions the contact with British sailors at Newcastle as a source of anarchist influence, Alvares Barata, "Revolta," 108.

93. And most probably, only in 1922 when the Brazilian Communist Party was founded. Silva, who studied the press coverage in Rio of the revolt, notes the weak links between the proletarian press and the sailors. See Marcos Silva, *Contra a chibata*, passim.

94. On the spread of radical ideologies among sailors on the Atlantic in the eighteenth and nineteenth centuries, see Linebaugh and Rediker, *Many-Headed Hydra*.

95. Hough, *Potemkin*, 190.

96. *Jornal do Comércio*, Nov. 26, 1910, 2.

97. The ideological influence of Brazil's Jacobins of the 1890s on the sailors of 1910 was next to none. The Jacobins' authoritarianism, ultranationalism, and xenophobia were irrelevant to the sailors' concerns.

98. Cândido, "Depoimento," 72, 92.

99. Liga, 5–6, Arquivo da Marinha.

100. Brazil, Hermes, *Relatório*, 1912, 104, reprinted in Brazil, Documentos Parlamentares, *Mensagens presidenciais*.

101. On these matters, see Needell, "Revolta," passim.

102. *Jornal do Comércio*, Nov. 26, 1910, 2: "A sublevação da Esquadra."

103. Arias Neto, "Em busca da cidadania," 222, 242.

104. Ibid., 342.

105. See Acemoglu et al., "Institutions," passim., on how the franchise in Britain determined access to education and the right to organize for the British working class, thereby advancing democracy. James Holston argues that in Brazil both the imperial constitution and that of the First Republic established equality before the law (abolishing aristocratic privileges) but not equality of rights. In Brazilian history, "the difference-based formula of citizenship overwhelms. It persists as a system of unequal and differential access to rights, privileges, and powers from the colonial period [to the present]." He also points out that Brazil was the last Latin American republic to permit illiterates to vote, in the constitution of 1988. Holston, *Insurgent Citizenship*, 27, 40, 102.

106. Arias Neto, "Em busca da cidadania," 352, 359, 365.

107. Velasco e Cruz, "Puzzling," 243.

108. Freyre, *Ordem*, II, 735.

109. Ibid., 736, citing Oficial, 78.

110. *Correio da Manhã*, Nov. 24, 1910, 2.

Chapter 4

1. Cândido, "Memórias," Jan. 8, 1913.

2. Nascimento, "Do convés," 38.

3. US Office of Naval Intelligence, "The Revolt" no. 76, 6. US National Archives.

4. Martins, "A revolta," 164.

5. E. Morel, *A revolta*, 3d ed., 160.

6. A bill was being drafted to definitively end corporal published two days before the second revolt (see below), but the eruption of the uprising of Dec. 9–10 may have brought about the indefinite tabling of the project. See Brazil. Congresso Nacional. Senado da República, "Indicação."

7. Nascimento, *Cidadania*, 243; Martins, "A revolta," 164. Cf. the fact that Brazilian slaves who could offer their masters their own market value could customarily obtain manumission, despite the fact that there was no statute requiring masters to grant it. Carneiro da Cunha, "Silences."

8. Italics in original.

9. Carew, *Lower Deck*, 31.

10. Ibid., 144.

11. Greenhalgh, *Presigangas*, 89.

12. Martins, "A revolta," 164, citing João Cândido's testimony during his trial.

13. Pereira da Cunha, *A revolta da esquadra*, 99–100. The author had participated in the suppression of the rebellion on the *Rio Grande do Sul*, noted below.

14. João B M. Pimentel [a seaman] to "querida madrinha," Dec. 8, 1910, in Conselho de Guerra, Nov. 30, 1912, 29–31, Arquivo Nacional.

15. Arias Neto, "Em busca da cidadania," 282.

16. Martins, "A revolta," 173, 182; Maestri, *Cisnes*, 96; Arias Neto, "Em busca da cidadania," 282; Braga, *1910*, 308.

17. The Corpo de Fuzileiros Navais was renamed the Batalhão Naval in 1908.

18. Capanema, "Être Noir," 6–7. Her sample included 20 percent of the total number of enlisted men in the Naval Battalion.

19. US Office of Naval Intelligence, "Revolt," 5, US National Archives.

20. Martins, "A revolta," 175.

21. Not to be confused with Francisco Marques da Rocha, commander of the Naval Battalion, or Naval Minister Marques de Leão.

22. Martins, "A revolta," 176. This claim is disputed by Maestri, who states that the majority did revolt, *Cisnes*, 97.

23. *O País*, Dec. 10, 1910, 2.

24. See below.

25. US Office of Naval Intelligence, "Revolt," 6, US National Archives.

26. The American Chargé in Rio, Dudley, says four to five hundred prisoners. Such numbers must have included seamen as well. Dudley to Secy of State, Dec. 16, 1910, letter, 4.

27. E. Morel, *A revolta*, 3d ed., 152.

28. Martins, "A revolta," 177.

29. Copy of letter to Secretary of State from Chargé Robert Woods Bliss, sent

by Dudley, including an extract from a letter by an unnamed British naval officer. See US Office of Naval Intelligence, Dudley to Secy of State, 3.

30. Pereira da Cunha, *A revolta da esquadra,* 106. Maestri, *Cisnes,* 98. Martins, "A revolta," 176.

31. Arias Neto, "Em busca da cidadania," 9.

32. In his testimony, Dias Martins concurred in this judgment. "Inquérito," 111–13, Arquivo Nacional. Cândido, "Memórias," Jan. 11, 1913.

33. Maestri, *Cisnes,* 98.

34. US Office of Naval Intelligence, "Revolt," 3.

35. Martins, "A revolta," 73.

36. Cândido, "Memórias," Jan. 9, 1913. Martins, "A revolta," 186.

37. Telegrams published in *Correio da Manhã,* Dec. 10, 1910, 1; and *O País,* Dec. 10, 1910, 2.

38. O País, Dec. 10, 1910, 2.

39. Martins, "A revolta," 185.

40. Maestri, *Cisnes,* 100; Martins, "A revolta," 185.

41. Cândido, "Memórias," Jan. 9, 1913.

42. Cândido, "Memórias," Jan. 9, 1913; Martins, "A revolta," 185.

43. Martins, "A revolta," 185.

44. He held the rank of Capitão-de-Fragata, just below Capitão-de-Mar-e-Guerra.

45. Martins, "A revolta," 186.

46. Pereira Leite also asked to be relieved of his new position. On both, see *O País,* Dec. 12, 1910, 2.

47. According to Cândido's "Memories," and his trial testimony in 1912—but not confirmed by other sources—a delegation of seamen personally went to Catete Palace to learn whether the president had really ordered them off the ship. Cândido, "Memórias," Jan. 10, 1913; Martins, "A revolta," 186. This action would obviously indicate a major breakdown in discipline.

48. Martins, "A revolta," 185–86.

49. Ibid., 197.

50. Bello, "Versão Oficial" [from a draft of his "Elementos"], published in E. Morel, *A revolta,* 5th ed., 327.

51. Martins, "A revolta," 187; Cândido, "Memórias," Jan. 7, 1913.

52. Bello, in E. Morel, *A revolta,* 5th ed., 327.

53. Martins, "A revolta," 186–87.

54. Capitão-de-Corveta.

55. Noronha Santos, Dec. 12, 1910, in Conselho de Guerra, 38–40, Arquivo Nacional. (Not to be confused with Júlio César de Noronha, minister of the navy, 1902–6).

56. Note that one source, Paulo, considers the sailors on the *Deodoro* the most militant during the first mutiny.
57. *Le Temps*, Nov. 26, 1910, 1; Dec. 12, 1910, 2; *New York Times*, Nov. 26, 1910, 3.
58. Martins, "A revolta," 190.
59. Arias Neto, "Em busca da cidadania," 280, n. 880.
60. Barbosa to Batista Pereira, Fazenda Rio das Pedras, Jan. 2, 1911, quoted in Viana Filho, *A vida de Rui Barbosa*, 486.
61. Ibid., 484.
62. US Office of Naval Intelligence, "Revolt," 8.
63. Brazil, Documentos Parlamentares, *Mensagens presidenciais*, 33.
64. Capanema, *Construction*, 88.
65. E. Morel, *A revolta*, 3d ed., 148.
66. US Office of Naval Intelligence, "Revolt," 10.
67. Dudley to Secy, Dec. 16, 1910, 5. The order for a third scout cruiser was probably canceled at the same time.
68. Maestri, *Cisnes*, 102.
69. Pereira da Cunha, *A revolta da esquadra*, 101; Maestri, *Cisnes*, 97.
70. The strategic importance of the island had been obvious to the French privateer Duguay-Trouin when he occupied Rio de Janeiro in 1711. He seized it as a military strongpoint. On recovering the city, the Portuguese incorporated the island into their defenses and completed the fort there in 1761.
71. Greenhalgh, *Presigangas*, 109.
72. João Cândido, quoted in E. Morel, *A revolta*, 3d ed., 181–82. Also see Cândido, "Memórias," Jan. 10, 1913; and Cândido, "Depoimento," 82–83.
73. The exact numbers of prisoners are in dispute, but it is agreed that only two men survived in Cândido's cell. My numbers are those given by Cândido himself, in an account he provided to the *Gazeta de Notícias* at the end of 1912. See issue of Jan. 10, 1913, 1.
74. *Diário das Notícias*, Dec. 28, 1910; *Correio da Manhã*, Jan. 17, 1911, reported in E. Morel, *A revolta*, 3d ed., 154–55.
75. The other survivor of the hecatomb in Cândido's cell was a marine, João Avelino Lira. Martins, "A revolta," 197.
76. Cândido interview by E. Morel, *A revolta*, 3d ed., 182; Cândido, "Memórias," Jan. 11, 1913.
77. *Correio da Manhã*, Feb. 20, 1911, 1.
78. "Insolação na Ilha das Cobras," in *Diário das Notícias*, Dec. 28, 1910.
79. Greenhalgh, *Presigangas*, 110.
80. Fonseca Filho, *Marechal Hermes*, 204. Brazil, Leão, *Relatório*, 22; J. M. Carvalho, "Os bordados," 73.
81. E. Morel, *A revolta*, 3d ed., 185.

82. Bello, "Elementos," 26; Cândido, "Memórias," Jan. 12, 1913; Marco Morel reproduces the letter by the psychiatrist who ascertained Cândido no longer was mentally disturbed in M. Morel, *João Cândido*.

83. For the early history of the prison colony, see Samis, *Clevelândia*. The site was named in honor of President Grover Cleveland (see Chapter 1).

Internal exile was not always limited to lower-class Brazilians. In 1893, during the revolt against President Floriano Peixoto, the government had sent a contingent of political prisoners to the Amazon, including top-ranking naval officers and imperial nobles. Arias Neto, "Em busca da cidadania," 200. For a history of the "undesirables" in Rio in the early republic, see Medeiros, *Indesejáveis*.

84. The younger man's attitude toward the lower classes is perhaps indicated by his alleged treatment of a maid, who was residing in another man's house several years later. In 1917 Flores was appointed provisional prefect of Uruguaiana, Rio Grande do Sul, a community bordering Uruguay; he simultaneously held the post of assistant police chief. Without a warrant, he ordered the girl to be brought to the stationhouse, ostensibly for interrogation, but possibly for other purposes as well. A court case against Flores was denied merit by the judge, appointed by the state party. See Estado do Rio Grande do Sul: Comarca de Uruguaiana. Cartório do Jury. Precesso Sumário de Justiça. Dr. José Antônio Flores da Cunha . . . [et alii]. C. do Civel e Crime Uruguaiana. No. 1526, maço 52, estante 83. [1917].

85. Storry, *Relatorio*, 1.

86. According to João Cândido, Vitalino had been one of the organizers of the planning sessions of the revolt in November 1910. During the rebellion, he had also been the second in command of the *Minas Gerais*. "Memórias," Jan. 6 and 7, 1913.

87. Storry, *Relatorio*, 1–2; Martins, "A revolta," 199. Martins gives a list of those executed.

88. Storry, *Relatorio*, 4.

89. On Rondon's work, see Diacon, *Stringing Together a Nation*.

90. Belfort to Rui Barbosa, May 30, 1911; Hardman, *Trem fantasma*, 157.

91. According to one source, the number of deaths of railroad workers as a share of the construction crews approached 10 percent in 1911. Ferreira, *A ferrovia*, 270.

92. See Storry's account, *Relatório*, 4.

93. Diacon, *Stringing Together a Nation*, 56.

94. Hardman, *Trem fantasma*, 159, says there was one female survivor, who received money to return to Rio. Belfort de Oliveira to Rui, May 30, 1911.

95. Belfort to Rui Barbosa, May 30, 1911.

96. Hardman, *Trem fantasma*, 163.

97. Hardman, *Trem fantasma*, 160, 248, citing Major Amílcar Botelho de Magalhães, *Impressões da Comissão Rondon*, 28.

98. Rivadavia Correia, from Pinheiro's Riograndense Republican Party, and Alexandrino Alencar (who had become minister in 1913), respectively.

99. Barbosa, "Requerimento," 8, 11–13.

100. Cândido, "Depoimento," 82.

101. Martins, "A revolta," 194.

102. Conselho de Guerra, "Mandado de Intimação," Arquivo da Marinha.

103. M. Morel, *João Cândido*, 77.

104. During the period in question, Brazil had no secular associations to defend the rights of black people. In the United States, the National Association for the Advancement of Colored People was only founded in 1909.

105. Martins, "A revolta," 201.

106. This was not precisely the truth. João Cândido received emissaries from the Naval Battalion rebels on the *Minas*, but he soon put them off again. Conselho de Guerra, 780, Arquivo Nacional.

107. "A sentença do Conselho de Guerra, lavrado pelo auditor dr. Bulcão Vianna." *Correio da Manhã*, Dec. 2, 1912, 2.

Chapter 5

1. The same was also true of Brazil's foremost novelist, Joaquim Maria Machado de Assis, though his criticism was subtler than the others', and usually took the form of irony. He died two years before the events related here.

2. José Eduardo de Macedo Soares. See Oficial da Armada, passim.

3. Ibid., *Política versus Marinha*.

4. Ibid., 55, 85–94, passim.

5. Ibid., 124, 127.

6. Arias Neto, "Em busca da cidadania," 291. Cf. "regeneracionismo" in late nineteenth-century Spain, a movement to discover the causes of Spain's decay as a nation and rectify them. Its most important writer was Joaquín Costa, who called for an "iron surgeon" to cure Spain's social and political maladies.

7. Batista das Neves, Relatório of May 2, 1910, cited in Capanema, "Nous, marins," 194.

8. Clemenceau, *Notes de voyage*, 216.

9. He also mentions class prejudice, but doesn't develop the argument. Bomílcar, *O preconceito*, 10.

10. Ibid., 14, 23, 45, 48.

11. Ibid., 28, 65, 96, 98.

12. Finot, *Race Prejudice*, 317. This statement is surprisingly in tune with modern anthropological notions about "social race," and it anticipates Franz Boas's more systematic investigation and similar conclusions by several years.

13. Bomílcar, *O preconceito*, 99.

14. Liga Marítima Brasileira, Arquivo da Marinha. "Promiscuidade" also means slovenliness or rowdiness, but I think promiscuity is meant here, and the sexual meaning is the first one given in the *Dicionário Aurélio* (http://www .dicionariodoaurelio.com/Promiscuidade).

15. Beattie, "Conflicting Penile Codes," 77.

16. Ibid., 73.

17. Caminha, *Bom-Crioulo*, 50, 100.

18. Green, *Beyond Carnival*, 22. In fact, sodomy had been decriminalized in the Code of 1830.

19. But not Freud.

20. Pires de Almeida, *Homossexualismo*, 163, 176, 178. Domingos Firmino Pinheiro presented a thesis at Bahia's School of Medicine in 1898 with a similar thrust: celibacy is impossible in males, and homosexuals acquire their sexual preferences for a variety of reasons—both hereditary and environmental. Homosexuality especially tends to be acquired in "religious communities, . . . in the navy, in the army, in preparatory schools and seminaries." Like Pires de Almeida, Pinheiro cited Krafft-Ebing and other contemporary European authorities. For him homosexuals were "victims . . . of sexual psycho-neuroses." Pinheiro, *Androphilismo*, 19, 26, 108, 184 (quotation).

21. Bello, "Elementos," 5.

22. J. M. Carvalho, "Os bordados," 74.

23. J. M. Carvalho, "Os bordados," 79. The youth in Figure 4 is Antônio Ferreira de Andrade, according to M. Morel, *João Cândido*, 56.

24. Freyre uses the term "cônegos" for the NCOs who were the patrons of young sailors. *Ordem*, vol. 1, cxxvi. Cf. "conegaço," probably a variant term, to denote "veteran sailor," and also meaning one who played the male role in a homosexual relationship. Arias Neto, "Em busca da cidadania," 343.

25. Romero, *Estudos sociaes*, 20, 21, 23.

26. Ibid., 9, 19.

27. Schwarcz, *O Espetáculo*, 153–54, citing Sílvio and Nelson Romero, *História da literatura brasileira* (Rio de Janeiro: J. Olympio, 1949).

28. Ibid., 208.

29. *O problema nacional brasileiro* and *A organisação nacional*.

30. On these matters, see Skidmore, *Black into White*.

31. Gaffre, *Visions du Brésil*, 36.

32. Freyre, II, 739; Leão, quoted in Martins, "A revolta," 207.

33. Pereira da Cunha, *A revolta da esquadra*, 28.

34. Arias Neto, "Em busca da cidadania," 311.

35. This is also the view of Admiral Juvenal Greenhalgh in *Presigangas*, 89.

36. Beattie, *Tribute*, 226–27 (on revolt of Dec. 1915); *Correio da Manhã*, Apr. 8, 1916, 3.

37. Fundo Delegacia Especial de Segurança Política e Social, "Viva 22 de novembro," Arquivo do Estado do Rio de Janeiro. Paulo, *Revolta*.

38. Capitani, *A rebelião*, 19, 23, 53, 65, 87.

39. On the complex issues of citizenship across Brazilian history and the differences in defining citizenship in the United States and Brazil, see Holston, *Insurgent Citizenship*.

40. Rodrigues, *Vozes do mar*, 174. Capitani, *A rebelião*, 70. The president of the sailors' association, José Anselmo dos Santos, was, however, an agent provocateur. See M. Morel, *João Cândido*, 97.

41. http://en.wikipedia.org/wiki/HMS_Agincourt_(1913)

42. Dantas Barreto, *Conspirações*, 208.

43. President Prudente de Morais was almost assassinated in 1897, when a soldier killed the minister of war accompanying the president. The assailant may have been motivated by Jacobin ideas or propaganda.

44. Martins, "A revolta," 208.

45. Viana Filho, *A vida do Barão do Rio Branco*, 458.

46. Nery, "Ziquiziras." Maria Eduarda Marques brought this term to my attention.

47. As noted above, the year of his death is uncertain. Bello thinks he died a drunkard; see Bello "Sucintos elementos," 12.

48. Fonseca Filho, 153.

49. E. Morel, *A revolta*, 5th ed., 85, n. 8.

50. E. Morel, *A revolta*, 3d ed., 216.

51. Ibid., 255. Other information from Cândido, "Depoimento."

52. Capanema, "Nous, marins," 427.

53. Ibid., 474.

54. The wording is inaccurate, since the "Golden Law" abolished the institution of slavery, and only by implication did it stop flogging.

Works Cited

Archival Sources

ABBREVIATIONS

AQO = Archives Diplomatiques du Quai d'Orsay, Paris
ARGS = Arquivo Público do Estado do Rio Grande do Sul, Porto Alegre
ARJ = Arquivo Público do Estado do Rio de Janeiro, Rio de Janeiro
AM = Arquivo da Marinha, Rio de Janeiro
AMNE = Arquivo do Ministério de Negócios Estrangeiros, Palácio das Necesidades, Lisboa
AN = Arquivo Nacional, Rio de Janeiro
CRB = Casa Rui Barbosa, Rio de Janeiro
NARA = National Archives and Records Administration, Washington, DC
TNA = The National Archives, London

Belfort de Oliveira to Rui Barbosa. 30 May 1911. CR 1072/2(2), CRB.
Bello, Luís Oliveira. "Elementos auténticos da vida do marinheiro João Cândido na Marinha de Guerra. Época—6 de janeiro de 1895 a 30 de dezembro de 1912." [Signed at end: L. de Oliveira Bello, 12 Jan. 1960]. Typescript from "Revolta da Armada" file. AM.
———. "Suscintos elementos auténticos da vida do ex-marinheiro João Cândido na Marinha de Guerra entre os anos de 1895–1912." Typescript in "Revolta da Armada" file. AM.
Brazil. Congresso Nacional. Senado da República dos Estados Unidos do Brasil, 7 Dec. 1910. "Indicação" doc. 86.1435, lata 162. AM.
"Caderneta subsidiária do livro de socorros pertenecente ao Marinheiro nacional da 16ª Companha 1ª classe, no. 85 João Cândido" Conselho da Guerra. *Inquérito*. 565/360–61, 344–55. AN.

Comarca de Uruguaiana. Cartório do Jury. Processo Sumário de Justiça. Dr. José Antônio Flores da Cunha . . . [et alii]. C. do Civel [sic] e Crime Uruguaiana. No. 1526, maço 52, estante 83. ARGS.

Conselho de Guerra. "Revolta da Chibata." 30 Nov. 1912 [originally cataloged in S. T. Militar, 7 Dec. 1912] new classification S.T.M./no. 565/caixa 13.789 AN.

———. "Mandado de Intimação do Rio" [document prepared by Dr. João Vicente Bulcão Viana, and signed by him.] Doc. 9715.134. Lata 159, dated 25 June 1912. AM.

Dodsworth Martins, [Almirante] Jorge. Memórias publicadas e anotadas por José Schiavo no "Jornal do Povo" Ponte Nova, MG, 1974–75. AM.

"Ex-marinheiro, um" to Comandante Luiz A. de Alencastro Graça, Rio, 5 Sept. 48. MS, doc. 1376, caixa 103. AM.

Fundo Delegacia Especial de Segurança Política e Social, Série Panfletos 1933–45. Documento 1090: "Viva 22 de novembro." ARJ.

Gabinete de Identificação da Marinha, Marinheiros Nacionais, Livros 1 and 2, 1908, AM.

Imperial and Foreign Intelligence [Great Britain]. Sir W[illiam] Haggard to Sir Edward Grey. 12 Dec. 1910. no. 126. "The Naval Mutiny in Rio: The Mutineers and the President." Minutes. FO 371/1051 4006. TNA.

"Inquérito da 3ª Delegacia Auxiliar para Averiguar as Causas que Motivaram a Revolta das Guarnições dos Couraçados Minas Gerais, São Paulo, Scout Rio Grande do Sul e Batalhão Naval." 24 Apr. 1912. GIFI 6C-385. AN.

Lacombe to Stéphen Pichon, Ministre français des Affaires Etrangères. Petrópolis, 28 Nov. 1910. Correspondance politique et commerciale, politique Intérieure - Immigration, vol. 6, juin-décembre 1910. AQO.

[Lacombe to Ministry]. Rio de Janeiro, 29 Nov. 1910. Correspondance politique et commerciale, politique Intérieure - Immigration, vol. 6, juin-décembre 1910. AQO.

Lacombe to Pichon. Petropolis. 15 Dec. 1910. Correspondance politique et commerciale, politique Intérieure - Immigration, vol. 6, juin-décembre 1910. AQO.

Lacurte Junior, Alberto. "Lotação de alguns navios da armada em 1910." Serviço de Documentação da Marinha. 20 Aug. 1948. Pasta 46. Number 2. Filed under "Revolta da Armada." AM.

Leão, Joaquim Marques. Untitled order to sink rebel ships: Rio, 25 Nov. 1910. Revolta da Esquadra, pasta 46, doc. 4. AM.

Liga Marítima Brasileira: 1910–1911. (Contains "Disciplina Abordo"). AM.

Negócios Estrangeiros. Direção Geral. Lisboa. 25 June 1910. No. 44. AMNE.

Storry, Carlos Brandão [Comandante]. *Relatório da viagem extraordinária feita pelo paquete "Satellite," deste porto, ao de S. Antônio de Rio Madeira, principiada em 25 de dezembro de 1910 e terminada em 4 de março de 1911, apresentado ao Sr. Gerente da Companhia Lloyd Brazileiro.* CRB.

US Department of State. Dudley to Division of Latin-American Affairs, Petrópolis, 23 Nov. [*sic*] 1910 (telegram). *National Archives Microfilm Publications, Microcopy No. 519: Records of the Department of State Relating to Internal Affairs of Brazil, 1910–1929*, Roll 1. Washington, DC: National Archives, 1961. NARA.

US Office of Naval Intelligence. Dudley to Secretary of State. Petrópolis. 29 Nov. 1910. No. 615. NARA.

———. no. 70. "Mutiny of the Brazilian Sailors" by Lt. John S. Hammond, 3d Field Artillery, American Military Attaché, Bs. As., Argentina. NARA.

———. Register 758. American Legation, Bs.As. 19 Dec. 1911. NARA.

———. Register 799, number 70. "Brazilian Naval Revolt, 1910" [Various sources and dates, 1910–11]. NARA.

———. "The Revolt of the Naval Battalion (Marine Infantry) on the Ilha das Cobras, Rio de Janeiro. December 9, 1910," by "B" [presumably Lt. John S. Hammond, Military Attaché in Buenos Aires], no. 76. NARA.

Newspapers/Periodicals

INTERNATIONAL PRESS

Collier's (New York)

Current Literature (New York)

The Economist (London)

Le Figaro (Paris)

Gil Blas (Paris)

The Independent (New York)

A Lucta (Lisbon)

Le Matin (Paris)

O Mundo (Lisbon)

The Nation (London)

New York Times (New York)

La Prensa (Buenos Aires)

Outlook (New York)

O Século (Lisbon)

The Spectator (London)

Le Temps (Paris)

The Times (London)

La Vie Maritime (Paris)

RIO DE JANEIRO PRESS

Careta

Correio de Manhã

Diário de Notícias

FonFon

Gazeta de Notícias

O Globo

Jornal do Brasil

Jornal do Commercio

O Malho

O Paiz

Published Sources and Theses

Acemoglu, Daron, Simon Johnson, and James A. Robinson. "Institutions as the Fundamental Cause of Long-Run Growth." December 2005. *Handbook of Economic Growth*, ed. Philippe Aghion and Stephen Durlauf. North Holland. *econ-www.mit.edu/faculty*. Accessed on Apr. 9, 2007.

Allen, Robert L. *The Port Chicago Mutiny*. Berkeley, CA: Heyday Books, 1993.

Alvares Barata, Antão. "Revolta dos Marinheiros em 1910." *Revista marítima brasileira* 82, nos. 4–6 (Apr.–Jun. 1962): 103–17.

Amado, Gilberto. *Mocidade no Rio e primeira viagem à Europa*. Rio de Janeiro: José Olympio, 1956.

Amuchástegui, Antonio Jorge Pérez. *Mentalidades argentinas, 1860–1930*. Buenos Aires: Editorial Universitaria de Buenos Aires, 1964.

Arias Neto, José Miguel. "Em busca da cidadania: Praças da Armada Nacional 1867–1910." PhD diss., Universidade de São Paulo, 2001.

Barbosa, Rui. "Requerimento de informações sobre o caso do Satélite—II" *Anais do Senado*. Dec. 17, 1914. Online at the Fundação Casa Rui Barbosa website, *http://www.casaruibarbosa.gov.br/*. Accessed on Feb. 19, 2011.

———. *Conspiracões*. Rio de Janeiro and São Paulo: F. Alves, 1917.

Beattie, Peter. "Conflicting Penile Codes: Modern Masculinity and Sodomy in the Brazilian Military, 1860–1916." In *Sex and Sexuality in Latin America*, ed. Daniel Balderston and Donna J. Guy. New York: New York University Press, 1997.

———. *The Tribute of Blood: Army, Honor, Race, and Nation in Brazil, 1864–1945*. Durham, NC: Duke University Press, 2001.

Bomílcar, Alvaro. *O preconceito de raça no Brazil*. Rio de Janeiro: n.p., 1916.

Braga, Cláudio da Costa. *1910: O fim da chibata: Vítimas ou Algozes*. Rio de Janeiro: n.p., 2010.

Brazil. Congresso Nacional. *Annaes do Senado Federal. 1–30 de Novembro de 1910.* Vol. 5. Rio de Janeiro: Imprensa Nacional, 1912.

———. Directoria Geral de Estatística. *Boletim commemorativo da Exposição Nacional de 1908.* Rio de Janeiro, 1908.

———. Documentos Parlamentares. *Mensagens presidenciais. Presidência Hermes da Fonseca 1910–1914.* Vol. 2. Rio de Janeiro: Typographia Jornal do Commercio, 1921.

———. *Estatística eleitoral.* Rio de Janeiro: Ministério de Agricultura, 1914.

———. Ministério da Marinha. [Joaquim Marques Baptista de Leão.] *Relatório apresentado ao Presidente da República dos Estados Unidos do Brazil . . . em Maio de 1911.* Rio de Janeiro: Imprensa Nacional, 1911.

———. Ministério da Marinha. [Júlio César da Noronha.] *Relatório apresentado ao Presidente da República pelo Vice-Almirante Júlio César da Noronha . . . em abril de 1904.* Rio de Janeiro: Imprensa Nacional, 1904.

———. Ministério da Marinha. [Manuel Ignacio Belfort Vieira.] *Relatório apresentado ao Presidente da República pelo Contra-Almirante Manuel Ignacio Belfort Vieira . . . em abril de 1912.* Rio de Janeiro: Imprensa Nacional, 1912.

———. *Relatório apresentada ao Presidente da República pela Vice-Almirante Júlio César da Noronha . . . em abril de 1905.* Rio de Janeiro: Imprensa Nacional, 1905.

Bretas, Marcos Luiz. *A guerra das ruas: Povo e polícia na cidade de Rio de Janeiro.* Rio de Janeiro: Arquivo Nacional, 1997.

Bryce, James. *South America: Observations and Impressions.* 2d ed. New York: Macmillan, 1916.

Caminha, Adolfo. *Bom-Crioulo: The Black Man and the Cabin Boy.* Trans. E. A. Lacey. San Francisco: Gay Sunshine Press, 1982.

Cândido, João. See under "Felisberto, João Cândido"

Capanema P. de Almeida, Sílvia. "La construction d'un événement: *La Revolta da Chibata* (Rio de Janeiro, 1910) dans ses antécédents, sa réception et sa mémoire." Ecole des Hautes Etudes en Sciences Sociales (June 2004).

———. "Être Noir, Brésilien et marin: Identités et citoyenneté dans le période post-abolitionniste (1888–1914)." In *De la démocratie raciale au multiculturalisme: Brésil, Amériques, Europe,* ed. Sílvia Capanema P. de Almeida and Anaïs Fléchet. Brussels: Peter Lang, 2009.

———. "A modernização do material e do pessoal da Marinha nas vésperas da revolta dos marujos de 1910: modelos e contradições." *Estudos históricos* 23, no. 45 (2010): 147–69.

———. "'Nous, marins, citoyens brésiliens et républicains': identités, modernité et mémoire de la révolte des matelots de 1910." PhD diss., l'École des Hautes Études en Sciences Sociales, 2009.

Capitani, Avelino Bioen. *A rebelião dos marinheiros.* Porto Alegre: Artes e Ofícios, 1997.

Carew, Anthony. *The Lower Deck of the Royal Navy 1900–1930: The Invergordon Mutiny in Perspective.* Manchester, UK: Manchester University Press, 1981.

Carneiro da Cunha, Manuela. "Silences of the Law: Customary Law and Positive Law on the Manumission of Slaves in 19th Century Brazil." *History and Anthropology* 1, no. 2 (1985): 427–43.

Carvalho, José Carlos de. *O livro da minha vida: Na guerra, na paz e nas revoluções 1847–1910.* Vol. 1, 317–414. Rio de Janeiro: Typographia Jornal do Commércio, 1912.

Carvalho, José Murilo de. *Os bestializados: O Rio de Janeiro e a República que não foi.* Rio de Janeiro: Cia. das Letras, 1987.

———. "Os bordados de João Cândido." *História, Ciências, Saúde—Manguinhos* 2, no. 2 (July–Oct. 1995): 68–84.

———. "Forças Armadas na Primeira República." In *História geral da civilizacão brasileira, tomo 3: O Brasil Republicano*, ed. Boris Fausto. Rio de Janeiro and São Paulo: Difel, 1977.

Caulfield, Sueann. "The Birth of Mangue: Race, Nation, and the Politics of Prostitution in Rio de Janeiro, 1850–1942." In *Sex and Sexuality in Latin America*, ed. Daniel Balderston and Donna J. Guy, 86–87. New York: New York University Press, 1997.

Classic Encyclopedia. "Baron Adolf Von Marschall Von Bieberstein." *http:// www.1911encyclopedia.org/Baron_Adolf_Von_Marschall_Von_Bieberstein.* Based on the 11th edition of the *Encyclopaedia Britannica*, published 1911. Accessed on Feb. 12, 2011.

Clemenceau, Georges. *Notes de voyage dans l'Amérique du Sud.* Paris: Hachette, 1911.

O Clube Naval. *Clube Naval.* Pamphlet acquired at Clube Naval, Rio de Janeiro, July 22, 2004.

Costa, Angela Marques da, and Lília Moritz Schwarcz. *1890–1914: No tempo das certezas.* São Paulo: Editora Schwarcz, 2000.

da Cunha, Euclides. *Os sertões: Campanha de Canudos.* São Paulo: Laemmert, 1903. Recently retranslated by Elizabeth Lowe as *Backlands: The Canudos Campaign.* New York: Penguin, 2009.

Dantas Barreto, [Emídio]. *Expedição a Matto Grosso: a revolução de 1906.* Rio de Janeiro: Laemmert, 1907. *http://hdl.handle.net/2027/uc1.b291514.* Accessed on Mar. 28, 2010.

Delano, Amasa. *A Narrative of Voyages and Travels in the Northern and Southern Hemisphere.* Boston: E. G. House, 1817.

Diacon, Todd A. *Stringing Together a Nation: Cândido Mariano da Silva Rondon and the construction of a modern Brazil, 1906–1910.* Durham, NC: Duke University Press, 2004.

Dias, Arthur. *O problema naval: Condições actuaes da marinha de guerra e seu papel nos destinos do paíz.* Rio de Janeiro: Officina da estatística, 1899.

Encyclopedia Britannica. 11th ed. Cambridge and New York: 1910–11.

Enders, Armelle. *Histoire de Rio de Janeiro.* Paris: Fayard, 2000.

Felisberto, João Cândido. "Depoimento" de João Cândido. In *João Cândido: O Almirante Negro.* Rio de Janeiro: Gryphus: Museu da Imagem e do Som, 1999.

———. "Memórias de João Cândido o marinheiro." *Gazeta de Notícias* (Dec. 31. 1912–Jan. 12, 1913): 1 (on each daily issue).

Ferreira, Manoel Rodrigues. *A ferrovia do diabo.* São Paulo: Melhoramentos, n.d.

Ferrez, Gilberto. "A Avenida e seu album." In Marc Ferrez, *O Album da Avenida Central: Um documento fotográfico da construção da Avenida Rio Branco, Rio de Janeiro, 1903–1906,* 13–33. São Paulo: Ex Libris, 1983.

Finot, Jean [alt. name Jean Pinot]. *Race Prejudice.* Trans. Florence Wade-Evans. Reprint, Miami, FL: Mnemosyne, 1969. (First published in England, 1907; Fr. orig., *Le préjugé des races.* Paris: Felix Alcan, 1905.)

Fonseca Filho, Hermes da. *Marechal Hermes: Dados para uma biografia.* Rio de Janeiro: Instituto Brasileiro de Geografia e Estatística, 1961.

Freyre, Gilberto. *Ordem e Progresso.* 2 vols. Rio de Janeiro: Olympio, 1959.

Gaffre, Louis-Albert. *Visions du Brésil.* Rio de Janeiro: F. Alves; Paris: Aillaud, Alves e Cia, 1912.

Green, James N. *Beyond Carnival: Male Homosexuality in Twentieth-century Brazil.* Chicago: University of Chicago Press, 1999.

Greenhalgh, [Admiral] Juvenal. *Presigangas e calabouças: prisões da marinha no século XIX.* [Rio de Janeiro]: Serviço de Documentação da Marinha, 1998.

Hardman, Francisco Foot. *Trem fantasma: A modernidade na selva.* São Paulo: Cia. das Letras, 1991.

Holston, James. *Insurgent Citizenship: Disjunctions of Democracy and Modernity in Brazil.* Princeton, NJ: Princeton University Press, 2008.

Hough, Richard. *The Potemkin Mutiny.* New York: Pantheon, 1961.

[Jane, Fred T.] *Jane's Fighting Ships.* 2d ed. London: Sampson Low Marston, 1914.

Kagan, Donald. *The Peloponnesian War.* New York: Penguin, 2004 [2003].

Keegan, John. *The First World War.* New York: Vintage, 2000.

Lambuth, David. "The Naval Comedy and Peace Policies in Brazil." *The Independent* [New York] 22 (Dec. 1910): 1431.

Levine , Robert M. *Vale of Tears: Revisiting the Canudos Massacre in Northeastern Brazil, 1893–1897.* Berkeley: University of California Press, 1992.

Lima Barreto, [Afonso Henriques de]. *Recordações do escrivão Isaías Caminha.* 8th ed. São Paulo: Brasilienese, 1981.

Linebaugh, Peter, and Marcus Rediker. *The Many-Headed Hydra: Sailors, Slaves, Commoners and the Hidden History of the Revolutionary Atlantic.* London: Verso, 2000.

Love, Joseph L. *Rio Grande do Sul and Brazilian Regionalism: 1882–1930.* Stanford: Stanford University Press, 1971.

Ludwig, Armin K. *Brazil: A Handbook of Historical Statistics.* Boston: G. K. Hall, 1985.

Machado, Maria Cristina Teixeira. *Lima Barreto: Um pensador social na Primeira República.* São Paulo: EUFG/EDUSP, 2002.

Maestri, Mário. *Cisnes negros: Uma história da revolta da chibata.* São Paulo: Editora Moderna, 2000.

Magalhães, Amílcar Botelho de. *Impressões da Commissão Rondon.* 5th ed., enlarged. São Paulo: Companhia Editora Nacional, 1942.

Magalhães, Raymundo. *Rui, o homem e o mito.* Rio de Janeiro: Editora Civilização Brasileira, 1965.

Mahan, Alfred Thayer. *The Influence of Sea Power Upon History, 1660–1783.* Boston: Little, Brown and Co., 1890. *http://www.gutenberg.org/etext/13529.* Accessed on Feb. 19, 2011.

Mantua, Simão de [pseud. for Antônio Gomes Carmo]. *Figurões vistos por dentro (Estudo de psychologia social brasileira).* São Paulo: Monteiro Lobato, 1921.

Martins, Hélio Leôncio. "A revolta dos marinheiros - 1910." In *História Naval Brasileira*, vol. 5, tomo 1 B. Rio de Janeiro: Ministério da Marinha, Serviço de Documentação da Marinha, 1997.

Martins Filho, João Roberto. *A marinha brasileira na era dos encouraçados, 1895–1910.* Rio de Janeiro: Fundação Getúlio Vargas, 2010.

Meade, Teresa A. *"Civilizing" Rio: Reform and Resistance in a Brazilian City 1889–1930.* University Park: Pennsylvania State University Press, 1997.

Medeiros de Menezes, Lená. *Os indesejáveis: Desclassificados da modernidade. Protesto, crime e expulsão na Capital Federal (1890–1930).* Rio de Janeiro: EdURJ, 1996.

Moraes Filho, Evaristo de. Preface to *A revolta da chibata*, by Edmar Morel. 3rd ed. Rio de Janeiro: Graal, 1979.

Morel, Edmar. *A revolta da chibata.* 3d rev. ed. Rio de Janeiro: Graal, 1979.

———. *A revolta da chibata.* 5th ed. enlarged. Rio de Janeiro: Graal, 2009.

Morel, Marco, ed. *João Cândido: A luta pelos direitos humanos.* Rio de Janeiro: n.p., 2008.

Morgan, Zachary Ross. "Legacy of the Lash: Blacks and Corporal Punishment in the Brazilian Navy, 1860–1910." PhD diss., Brown University, 2001.

Nascimento, Álvaro P. do. *Cidadania, cor e disciplina na revolta dos marinheiros de 1910.* Rio de Janeiro: FAPERJ: Maud X, 2008.

————. "Do convés ao porto: A experiência dos marinheiros e a revolta de 1910." PhD diss., UNICAMP, 2002.

————. "Marinheiros em revolta: Recrutamento e disciplina na Marinha de Guerra (1880–1910)." MA thesis, UNICAMP, 1997. Revised and published as *A ressaca da marujada: recrutamento e disciplina na Armada Imperial.* Rio de Janeiro: Presidência da República, Arquivo Nacional, 2001.

National Maritime Museum. "Research guide B8: The Spithead and Nore mutinies of 1797." Apr. 2008. *http://www.nmm.ac.uk/server/show/conWebDoc.585/ setPaginate/No.* Accessed on Mar. 13, 2010.

"Navios de Guerra Brasileiros: 1822–hoje." *http://www.naviosdeguerrabrasileiros. hpg.ig.com.br/NGB-New.htm.* Accessed on Oct. 30, 2008.

Needell, Jeffrey D. "The Revolta Contra Vacina of 1904: The Revolt Against 'Modernization' in Belle Époque Rio de Janeiro." *Hispanic American Historical Review* 67, no. 2 (May 1987): 233–69.

————. *A Tropical Belle Epoque: Elite Culture and Society in Turn-of-the-Century Rio de Janeiro.* Cambridge: Cambridge University Press, 1987.

Nery, Sebastião. "As ziquiziras de Urucubaca." *Notícias da Bahia.* Aug. 21, 2008. *http://noticiasdabahia.com.br/colunas.php?cod=638* Accessed on Dec. 18, 2010.

Oficial da Armada, Um. [José Eduardo de Macedo Soares]. *Política versus Marinha.* Rio de Janeiro: Garnier, n.d.

Otoni, Cristiano Benedito. *Autobiografia.* Brasília: Editora Universidade de Brasília, 1983.

Paulo, Benedito [pseudonym for Pereira Nunes, Adão Manoel]. *A revolta de João Cândido.* Porto Alegre: Independência, 1934.

Pereira da Cunha, Heitor. *A revolta da esquadra brasiliera em novembro e dezembro de 1910.* Rio de Janeiro: Imprensa Naval, 1953. Reprint from *Revista Marítima Brasileira,* Oct.–Dec. 1949.

Pinheiro, Domingos Firmino. *O Androphilismo.* Bahia: Imprensa Económica, 1898. Medical thesis at the Faculdade de Medicina da Bahia. [I was not able to consult this document directly, but relied on the notes of Professor Dain Borges, who kindly lent them to me.]

Pires de Almeida, José Ricardo. *Homossexualismo (A libertinagem no Rio de Janeiro): Estudos sobre as perversões e inversões do instincto genital.* Rio de Janeiro: Lammaert, 1906.

Poder Naval & Marítimo. "Bem-Vindo ao Poder Naval Online." *http://www. naval .com.br.* Accessed on Oct. 30, 2008.

Queiroz, Suely Robles Reis de. *Os radicais da República.* São Paulo: Brasiliense, 1986.

Rio, João do [Pseudonym for Paulo Barreto]. *A alma encantadora das ruas.* Paris: H. Garnier, 1910 [1908].

Rodrigues, Flávio Luís. *Vozes do mar: O movimento dos marinheiros e o golpe de 64*. São Paulo: Cortez Editora, 2004.

Rodrigues, João Carlos. *João do Rio: Uma biografia*. Rio de Janeiro: Topbooks, 1996.

Romero, Sílvio, and Arthur Guimarães. *Estudos sociaes: O Brasil na primeira década do século XX*. Lisboa: Typ. da "A Editora," 1911.

Samis, Alexandre. *Clevelândia: Anarquismo, sindicalismo e repressão política no Brasil*. São Paulo: Imaginaria, 2002.

Scheina, Robert L. *Latin America: A Naval History*. Anapolis, MD: Naval Institute, 1987.

Schwarcz, Lília Moritz. *O espetáculo das raças: Cientistas, instituições e questão racial no Brasil: 1870–1930*. São Paulo: Cia. das Letras, 1993.

Scott, James C. *Seeing Like a State: How Certain Schemes to Improve the Human Condition Have Failed*. New Haven, CT: Yale University Press, 1999.

Serrão, Joel, and A. H. de Oliveira Marques. *Nova história de Portugal*. Vol. 11: *Portugal: Da monarquia à república*. Lisboa: Presença, 1991.

Silva, Eduardo da. *As queixas do povo*. Rio de Janeiro: Paz e Terra, 1988.

Silva, Marcus A. da. *Contra a chibata: Marinheiros brasileiros em 1910*. São Paulo: Brasiliense, 1982.

Skidmore, Thomas E. *Black into White: Race and Nationality in Brazilian Thought*. Durham, NC: Duke University Press, 1993.

Solis, Sidney Sérgio, and Marcus Venício Ribeiro. "O Rio onde o sol não brilha: acumulação e pobreza na transição para o capitalismo." *Revista Rio de Janeiro* 1, no. 1 (Sept./Dec. 1985): 45–59.

Souza e Silva, [Augusto Carlos de]. *Assumptos navaes*. Rio de Janeiro and Paris: H. Garnier, 1910.

Stepan, Nancy L. *Beginnings of Brazilian Science: Oswaldo Cruz, Medical Research and Policy, 1890–1920*. New York: Science History Publications, 1976.

Topik, Steven C. *Trade and Gunboats: The United States and Brazil in the Age of Empire*. Stanford: Stanford University Press, 1996.

Tuchman, Barbara W. *The Proud Tower: A Portrait of the World Before the War, 1890–1914*. New York: Macmillan, 1966.

Velasco e Cruz, María Cecilia. "Puzzling out Slave Origins in Rio de Janeiro Port Unionism: The 1906 Strike and the Sociedade de Resistência dos Trabalhadores em Trapiche e Café." *Hispanic American Historical Review* 16, no. 2 (May 2006): 205–45.

Viana Filho, Luís. *A vida do Barão do Rio Branco*. Porto: Lello & Irmao, 1983.

———. *A vida de Rui Barbosa*. [Salvador]: Academia de Letras da Bahia, [2008].

Index

Acre, 6, 8, 14, 69, 100–104
Adamastor, 26–27, 28, 31, 80
Adolfo Gordo Law, 6
Albuquerque, Francisco Monteiro de, 29, 34, 104
Albuquerque Lins, Manuel, 11
Alencar, Alexandrino de: as minister of the navy, 16–17, 27, 68–69, 73, 81, 129n12; relationship with João Cândido, 68–69; relationship with Hermes da Fonseca, 27, 44; relationship with Pinheiro Machado, 16–17
Alliance of National Liberation, 111
Alvares Barata, Antão, 132n92
Alves da Silva, José, 95, 124n32, 130n32
Amado, Gilberto, 13, 14, 19, 74–75
Amazonas, 23–24, 44, 87, 97, 102–3
Amistad, ix
amnesty, 37–43, 59, 74, 76, 87, 103, 104, 116; attitudes of officers regarding, 35, 97, 125n78; attitudes of rebels regarding, 88–89, 94, 96, 128n139; negotiated by José Carlos de Carvalho, 37–38, 39, 41, 42–43, 45, 46–47, 72
anarchism, 82, 132n92
apprenticeship schools, 21, 22, 84, 107
Aquidabã, 19, 27, 44
Araújo, José, 30
Argentina: attitudes of Brazilians regarding, 1–2, 3, 4, 5, 7, 16, 17, 20; Avenida de Mayo, 3; Buenos Aires, 1–2, 3, 78; immigrants to, 110; navy of, 19, 35, 77–78, 97; relations with Brazil, 8, 20, 35; Teatro Colón, 3

Arias Neto, José Miguel, 110, 128n139, 137n83
Armstrong-Whitworth Shipbuilding, 82
Army. *See* Brazilian army
Association of Sailors and Marines, 112
Austria-Hungary, 19–20, 121n99
Avelino, André, 53, 54, 95, 130nn24,26,32
Avelino Lira, João, 136n75
Azeredo, Antônio, 47

Babilônia, 28
Bahia, 71–72, 85; appearance, 55; armament, 20; in Buenos Aires, 67, 78; in Chile, 78, 80; during first revolt, 28, 30, 31, 35, 38, 45, 46–47, 55, 130n26; in Lisbon, 24, 25; during second revolt, 89, 92, 95
Bahia state, 11, 12, 113, 114
Bakunin, Mikhail, 82
Barbosa, Rui, 9–10; and Companhia Correcional, 66; in election of 1910, 11–12, 23, 39–40, 119n50; during first revolt, 28, 38–40, 41–42; "Lesson of the Far East," 9; on the navy, 9; relationship with Pinheiro Machado, 12, 13, 14, 96; and *Satélite* scandal, 102, 103; at Second Hague Peace Conference, 8, 10; during second revolt, 96, 127n120
Barreto, Paulo. *See* Rio, João do
Barroso, 35, 91
Batista das Neves, João, 17, 34, 73, 80, 106; death in first revolt, 28–29, 32, 47, 73, 74, 88, 89, 104; physical appearance, 49
Belfort de Oliveira, Booz, 102